the vegetarian pantry

the vegetarian pantry

fresh and modern recipes for meals without meat

chloe coker and jane montgomery

photography by **william reavell**

LONDON · NEW YORK

Dedication
For our mums, who made the kitchen home.

Senior Designer Sonya Nathoo
Photographic Art Direction
Megan Smith
Editor Ellen Parnavelas
Production Gary Hayes
Editorial Director Julia Charles
Art Director Leslie Harrington

Prop Stylist Jo Harris
Home Economists Chloe Coker and
Jane Montgomery
Food Stylist Rosie Reynolds
Indexer Hilary Bird

First published in the UK in 2013
by Ryland Peters & Small
20–21 Jockey's Fields
London WC1R 4BW
and
519 Broadway, 5th Floor
New York, NY 10012
www.rylandpeters.com

10 9 8 7 6 5 4 3 2 1

ISBN: 978-1-84975-344-9

A CIP record for this book is available
from the British Library.

Library of Congress Cataloging-in-
Publication Data has been applied for.

Printed in China

notes

• All spoon measurements are level unless otherwise specified.

• All butter is unsalted unless otherwise specified.

• All eggs are medium (UK) or large (US), unless otherwise specified. It is recommended that free-range, organic eggs be used whenever possible. Recipes containing raw or partially cooked egg, or raw fish or shellfish, should not be served to the very young, very old, anyone with a compromised immune system or pregnant women.

• When a recipe calls for the grated zest of citrus fruit, buy unwaxed fruit and wash well before use. If you can only find treated fruit, scrub well in warm soapy water and rinse before using.

• Ovens should be preheated to the specified temperatures. All ovens work slightly differently. We recommend using an oven thermometer and suggest you consult the maker's handbook for any special instructions, particularly if you are cooking in a fan-assisted/convection oven, as you will need to adjust temperatures according to manufacturer's instructions.

• Cheeses started with animal rennet are not suitable for strict vegetarians so read food labelling carefully and, if necessary, check that the cheese you buy is made with a non-animal (microbial) starter. Traditional Parmesan is not vegetarian so we recommend a vegetarian hard cheese (such as Gran Moravia which has the same texture so is ideal for grating) or Parma (a vegan product). There is an increasing number of manufacturers who are now producing vegetarian versions of traditionally non-vegetarian cheeses, such as Gruyère or Gorgonzola. Check online for suppliers and stockists in your location.

contents

introduction

We love nothing more than roaming around the local farmers' market or even the supermarket to look at the fresh produce on offer. Whatever the time of year, you will find an abundance of vegetables and fruit in varying colours, sizes and textures – from earthy potatoes and crooked carrots to colourful squashes and many varieties of tomatoes. Add to this the many grains, beans, nuts and seeds, along with fresh and dried herbs and preserved fruits that you can buy and you will have a well-stocked natural store cupboard, full of ingredients for an unlimited amount of tasty dishes at your finger tips.

Ironically, this is often not the perception of vegetarian cuisine. Although there is wonderful meat-free food out there, vegetarian food is often thought to be stodgy, uninspiring and complicated. In our opinion this could not be further from the truth. A bad example is never the only example but a bad example can put people off for life.

So why are we writing this book? Neither of us are strict vegetarians but we are both passionate about fresh, healthy, seasonal meat-free cooking. Chloe, whose mother has been vegetarian for over 40 years, grew up in a vegetarian kitchen. Jane was looking for interesting meat-free recipes both for herself and her clients but couldn't find the inspiration and ideas she was hoping for. Shared frustrations over a cup of tea led to a plan to put together a book of simple and flavourful recipes that did not cost the earth and would appeal to everyone – from traditional vegetarian cooks like Chloe's mother to meat-eaters, like Jane's clients, who were looking for something new.

Our aim is not to preach, patronize or convert – it is simply to share our passion for fresh, seasonal food and to give you ideas, encouragement and confidence in the kitchen, whether you are a strict vegan or vegetarian, a meat-eater who wants a more varied diet or someone who has a vegetarian coming for dinner and has no idea where to begin. We hope to provide you with the tools, confidence and inspiration to embrace this fantastic cuisine and try something new that you haven't made before.

The recipes in this book are focused on everyday home cooking and simple entertaining – with fresh ideas for every style of occasion – from a relaxed brunch or drinks party with friends, to light lunches and speedy weeknight suppers for the family. All of the recipes are designed as a starting point for your own kitchen and are easy to adjust to your particular tastes and dietary preferences, the ingredients you have in your store cupboard and fridge, or the fresh seasonal produce that catches your eye in the shop or at the market.

Where possible we have tried to cater for different dietary needs and included some vegan and gluten-free options. Many of the recipes can be easily adjusted to suit your requirements – dairy foods can often simply be omitted (where they are serving suggestions) and wheat (or other gluten-containing ingredients) can be substituted with readily available gluten-free alternatives so that everyone can use and enjoy our book.

Chloe & Jane

the healthy vegetarian

There are many definitions of a vegetarian diet and many reasons why people choose to follow the diet that they do: ethical, environmental, health, religious, financial or simply personal choice. Vegetarian diets can be either simply meat-free or some people may choose to also exclude either eggs or dairy (or both), or eat a totally vegan diet, free from all animal products, including honey. It is important that when food groups are removed from a person's diet, the balance of key dietary components are considered and maintained.

what is a vegetarian diet?

There is no single definition of a vegetarian diet. Some include dairy and eggs (lacto-ovo vegetarian), whilst others may exclude dairy but eat eggs or vice versa. For the purposes of this book we have taken a broad approach to what is a vegetarian diet, including dairy and eggs. Where we have used products such as cheese and wine, vegetarian products are available. Should you follow a stricter diet, the recipes are designed to be easily adapted to suit your needs and eggs and dairy are often included as serving suggestions only.

A vegan diet does not contain any foods of animal origin such as dairy, gelatine or honey. This book contains a number of vegan recipes. Many of the recipes can also be amended for a vegan diet, either by omitting ingredients or substituting with vegan alternatives such as soya/soy-based products. These recipes are indicated with a (v) symbol.

Whilst gluten-free diets are not part of vegetarian cuisine, they are becoming more prevalent and can easily be catered for with a little thought. Whilst most people are aware that gluten is found in foods containing wheat-based products, it can also be found in unexpected places such as ice cream, tomato ketchup and baking powder. We have included a number of gluten-free recipes in this book and these are indicated with a (x) symbol. Gluten-free alternatives to everyday foods and cooking ingredients are now widely available, or try substituting wheat-based flours with alternatives such as gram (chickpea) flour.

Just as what it means to be vegetarian can vary widely, so can the associated nutritional needs of each vegetarian diet. While a well-balanced vegetarian diet can be a healthy choice (they are often low in saturated fat and cholesterol and naturally high in fibre/fiber and antioxidants), if not well balanced, they can be lacking in essentials such as protein, iron, omega 3, calcium and certain vitamins (in particular vitamins D and B12). This is especially true of some vegan diets. As such, extra care must be taken to make sure that an individual's diet is well balanced and nutritionally complete by ensuring that it contains a balance of food naturally rich in particular nutrients or, where necessary, including some fortified foods.

Those feeding children, expectant mothers and elderly people should take extra care to ensure that their diets are well-balanced.

key nutrients in the vegetarian diet

CARBOHYDRATE AND FIBRE/FIBER are usually plentiful in a good vegetarian or vegan diet – eating a variety of fruit and vegetables, including skins where possible, along with bran, potatoes and wholegrains should provide everything needed.

PROTEIN is essential in any diet. Not only is it necessary to the body for growth and repair and the production of enzymes and hormones, it also makes you feel full. An average person should eat around 45–55 g/1½–2 oz. of protein a day. In a meat-free diet, it can be harder to find complete sources of protein. This can be combatted by ensuring that you eat a variety of foods during the day and by mixing different sources of protein in one dish, such as grains with pulses, nuts or seeds. Whilst soya/soy, eggs, milk and cheese are all excellent sources of protein, they can be over-used. Consider using a variety of lentils, beans, chickpeas and wholegrains in your cooking – these are often interchangeable in a recipe so just use what you have in the pantry. Quinoa is a good source of protein added to salads or used as a substitute for rice. A sprinkling of chopped nuts or seeds is a great way to add extra protein to any dish.

KEY VITAMINS AND MINERALS can sometimes be lacking in vegetarian diets. As well as what you are eating, think about the cooking process – try to eat a substantial amount of raw vegetables or use cooking methods such as steaming and blanching to retain as much goodness as possible. As well as eating a broad range of fruit and vegetables, for those who eat dairy and/or eggs, a lot of essential vitamins (A, B2, B12 and D) can be found in milk and eggs. For those who do not eat dairy, fortified foods such as breakfast cereals and soya/soy milk are good sources of vitamins, as are green vegetables. Vitamin C, found in citrus fruit, is usually plentiful in vegetarian and vegan diets. Not only is it important for the body, it also helps to release minerals from pulses and vegetables and helps the body to absorb iron – try squeezing some lemon juice over a salad or adding it to a dressing.

CALCIUM can easily be found in dairy produce, but those following a dairy-free diet should ensure that they include plenty of green vegetables (such as kale and broccoli), sesame seeds, beans and nuts in their diet. Calcium can also be found in soya/soy milk and fruit juices.

IRON can be lacking in meat-free diets, but eating a combination of leafy green vegetables, dried fruits, beans, nuts, seeds and tofu will combat this.

FATTY ACIDS generally vegetarian diets are fairly low in saturated fat. Dairy products are a good source of fatty acids, although it is important not to be over-reliant on them. Seeds, walnuts and soya/soy are good sources of fat. Why not also try using different oils – nut oils, rapeseed and linseed oils can all be used both for cooking and flavouring.

HAPPINESS Some things in your diet should be used to simply to feed the soul and make you feel good. Cakes, for example, have little nutritional value but they certainly put a smile on your face!

the well-stocked vegetarian pantry

A well-stocked store cupboard is a great starting point for creating exciting vegetarian dishes every day of the week – whether you are trying something new or need a quick solution. Here is a basic guide to what we always keep in stock:

in the store cupboard

BAKING SUPPLIES
Flours · Plain/all-purpose flour, strong bread flour, wholemeal/wholewheat flour and gram flour
Raising agents · Fast-action yeast, baking powder and bicarbonate of soda/baking soda

SWEET THINGS
Sugars · Brown sugar and granulated/caster sugar
Chocolate · Dark/bittersweet chocolate (70% cocoa)
Honey and syrups · Honey, agave syrup, golden syrup/light corn syrup and maple syrup
Vanilla · Good-quality vanilla extract, vanilla bean paste or dried vanilla beans

GRAINS AND PULSES
Grains · Rice, wild rice, barley, bulgur wheat, quinoa, couscous and rolled oats
Pulses/legumes · Dried green, red and puy lentils, dried or canned kidney beans, butter beans and chickpeas

DRIED FRUIT, NUTS AND SEEDS
Dried fruit · Sultanas/golden raisins and apricots
Nuts · Ground almonds, flaked almonds, walnut halves, hazelnuts and pine nuts
Seeds · Sesame and poppy seeds

PRESERVED VEGETABLES
Tomatoes · Canned chopped tomatoes and passata, tomato purée/paste
Dried vegetables · Sun-dried tomatoes, porcini mushrooms
Jarred vegetables · artichokes, olives and capers

OILS AND VINEGARS
Cooking oils · Olive, canola/rapeseed and vegetable
Oils for drizzling · Extra virgin olive oil, sesame oil, walnut oil, hazelnut oil and truffle oil
Vinegars · White, red and sherry wine vinegars and good quality balsamic vinegar

HERBS AND SPICES
Fresh · Basil, mint, coriander/cilantro, rosemary, thyme, sage and flat-leaf parsley (ideally growing fresh in pots)
Dried herbs · Oregano, rosemary and thyme
Spices · Dried chilli/hot red pepper flakes, smoked paprika (pimentòn), cinnamon, turmeric, cumin and nutmeg

OTHER SEASONINGS
Good quality stock cubes or bouillon powder
Mustards · Dijon, English and wholegrain mustard
Salt and black pepper · Freshly ground is always best and stock sea salt flakes as well as table salt
Spice pastes · Fresh ginger, garlic, chilli/chile (minced or puréed), ready-made curry paste, harissa, etc

in the fridge and freezer

DAIRY ETC.
Eggs · Organic and free-range, whenever possible
Butter · Both salted and unsalted for baking
Cheese · Parmesan, Cheddar, feta and halloumi (started with non-animal rennets if preferred)
Tofu · Plain, marinated and smoked

FROZEN FRUIT AND VEGETABLES
Vegetables · Spinach, peas, broad/fava beans and edamame (fresh soya/soy beans)
Berries · 'Fruits of the forest' red berry mix

OTHER FROZEN FOODS
Pastry etc · Frozen all-butter puff and filo/phyllo sheets, Gyoza or dumpling wrappers

safe storage

When planning your store cupboard, think about what makes food spoil – bacteria, heat, air, light and moisture can all ruin ingredients. Here are a few tips on successful storage and remember to clear out your cupboard regularly so that expensive ingredients don't get lost in a dark corner.

CONTAINERS

Glass, tin, ceramic and lidded plastic containers are perfect for storing dry ingredients such as rice, beans, lentils, nuts, flours and cereals. Make sure that the containers are completely clean and dry, airtight with a good seal, and are clearly labelled with the contents and best-before date. If possible, store them in a cool, dark place with a constant temperature.

PRESERVING

Make the most of seasonal produce by making jams, pickles and chutneys. It's very satisfying to bottle summer fruits and berries in sugar syrups and brandies to enjoy during the winter months. Make sure that your jars are correctly sterilized and store them at an even temperature in a cool, dark place. Try our recipes for Sweet Chilli Jam (page 66) and Homemade Ketchup (page 64).

FREEZING

You can extend the shelf life of many ingredients by keeping them in the freezer. Nuts, seeds, fresh herbs and ground spices all freeze well. Keeping more unusual ingredients such as curry leaves and dumpling wrappers in the freezer means that you always have them to hand. You can also plan ahead with your cooking – make an extra batch of pastry or bread to freeze or have a few essential dishes ready in the freezer such as the Vegetable and Lentil Moussaka (page 99) or the Vegetable Tagine (page 104). Extra vegetables can also be frozen – why not make any leftover tomatoes into a quick sauce to keep in the freezer? Or chop any leftover fresh herbs and freeze them suspended in water in ice-cube trays.

breakfast and brunch

Breakfast is the most important meal of the day so start the day well with one of these deliciously satisfying options. Whether it is a grab-and-go muffin on the way to work, a leisurely brunch with friends or breakfast for one with coffee and the newspaper, here you'll find a recipe to suit every morning.

quick cornbread

There are lots of different ways to make cornbread and many different ingredients you can add to it. Below is the basic recipe that we like to use, along with the additions that we think are really tasty. Feel free to experiment as this recipe works just as well plain or made with different herbs and cheeses.

260 g/1⅔ cups polenta/
    cornmeal
75 g/scant ⅔ cup plain/
    all-purpose flour
1½ teaspoons baking powder
1 teaspoon salt
1 teaspoon sugar
100 g/scant ½ cup light brown
    soft sugar
1 egg
360 ml/1⅓ cups milk
5 tablespoons vegetable oil
1 roasted red (bell) pepper, diced
kernels from 1 cooked corn cob or
    180 g/⅔ cup canned or frozen
    sweetcorn kernels
1 fresh red chilli/chile, finely diced
2 teaspoons dried chilli/hot red
    pepper flakes
1½ tablespoons fresh parsley,
    roughly chopped
30 g/1 oz. feta or goat cheese,
    crumbled
butter, to serve (optional)

*a medium-size loaf pan, lined with
    parchment paper*

Serves 4–6

Preheat the oven to 200°c (400°F) Gas 6.

Put the polenta/cornmeal, flour, baking powder, salt and sugars in a mixing bowl and stir to combine. In a separate bowl, combine the egg, milk and oil and whisk lightly. Make a well in the centre of the dry ingredients. Pour in the egg mixture and stir to combine.

Add the red pepper, sweetcorn, chilli/chile, dried chilli/hot red pepper flakes, parsley and cheese and mix well.

Pour the mixture into the prepared loaf pan and bake in the middle of the preheated oven for 25–30 minutes, until a skewer inserted into the middle comes out clean.

Cut into slices and serve as they are or spread with butter or cream cheese, if liked. This cornbread is also delicious served with scrambled eggs.

potato and celeriac rosti with spinach and mushrooms and a poached egg

Rosti are much like hash browns and make a fantastic brunch dish topped with a poached egg, but you can omit the egg for vegans. We like the celeriac here but these are equally good made with parsnips, onions, carrots or beetroot.

200 g/7 oz. potatoes, scrubbed and halved
200 g/7 oz. celeriac/celery root, peeled and cut into large chunks
5 tablespoons olive oil
320 g/5–6 cups sliced chestnut or portobello mushrooms
1 garlic clove, crushed
100 g/1¾ cups baby spinach, washed, dried and finely chopped
2 eggs, chilled (optional)
truffle oil, for drizzling (optional)
salt and freshly ground black pepper

Serves 2–4

Preheat the oven to 180°C (350°F) Gas 4.

Bring a large saucepan of water to the boil and boil the potatoes for 6 minutes, until they start to soften. Drain and cool. Bring another large saucepan of water to the boil and add the celeriac/celery root. Boil for 5 minutes until it starts to soften slightly. Drain and set aside to cool.

Grate the potatoes and celeriac with a coarse grater, stir through 2 tablespoons of the oil and season well with salt and pepper.

Heat 2 more tablespoons of the oil in a large frying pan/skillet set over medium–high heat. Put a large spoonful of the rosti mixture into the pan and flatten it down well to a thickness of 1 cm/⅜ inch. Cook the rosti for 2–3 minutes on each side until crisp and golden. Repeat until all the rosti mixture is used up – you may need to cook them in batches if there is not enough room in the pan. Transfer the fried rosti to the oven and bake for 5 minutes.

Meanwhile, heat the remaining tablespoon of oil in a separate frying pan/skillet. Add the mushrooms and garlic and cook over medium heat until golden. Season with salt and pepper and stir in the spinach to wilt.

When the rosti are ready, poach the eggs, if using. Bring a saucepan of water to the boil, turn the heat down to a simmer and stir the water with a spoon to make a whirlpool. As the whirlpool dies, crack an egg into the centre of the pan. Cook the egg for about 3 minutes until the white is set but the yolk is still runny. Remove the egg from the pan with a slotted spoon and drain well.

Put the rosti on serving plates and top with the mushrooms and spinach. Finish with the poached eggs, a drizzle of truffle oil, if liked, and a generous grinding of black pepper.

saffron and pepper frittata with roasted garlic aioli

This frittata is bursting with Mediterranean flavour. If you don't have time to make the aioli yourself, simply stir the roasted garlic through a jar of good quality store-bought mayonnaise and it will be almost as delicious.

200 g/7 oz. Desiree potatoes, peeled
2 tablespoons olive oil
½ white onion, finely sliced
1 garlic clove, crushed
a pinch of smoked paprika
a handful of frozen peas, defrosted
100 g/½ cup roasted red peppers (you can roast them and skin them yourself or buy jars of antipasti roasted peppers)
4 eggs
a pinch of saffron strands, soaked in 1 tablespoon hot water

For the aioli
1 garlic bulb, unpeeled
50 ml/¼ cup olive oil
1 egg yolk
100 ml/scant 1 cup vegetable oil
a squeeze of fresh lemon juice
salt and freshly ground black pepper

Serves 4

Preheat the oven to 200°C (400°F) Gas 6.

To make the aioli, remove the outer skin from the garlic bulb but leave the skin around the individual cloves intact. Cut about 1 cm/½ inch off the top of the garlic bulb so that the tops of the garlic cloves are exposed. Put the garlic, exposed cloves upwards, in the centre of a piece of kitchen foil. Drizzle with 2 tablespoons of the olive oil, then fold the foil around it to make a parcel. Bake for 30–40 minutes until soft. Allow to cool slightly before squeezing the cloves out of their skins into a bowl. Mash with a fork.

Put the egg yolk in a small bowl with a pinch of salt. Slowly start to add the vegetable oil, drop by drop whisking constantly until it is all used up. Repeat with the remaining olive oil. If the mayonnaise becomes too thick, add a little lemon juice to thin it out. Stir in the garlic and season to taste with salt, pepper and a little more lemon juice. Cover and chill until needed.

To make the frittata, boil the potatoes in salted water until just cooked. Drain and let cool before slicing thinly.

Preheat the grill/broiler to medium. Heat 2 tablespoons of the olive oil in a frying pan/skillet with a heatproof handle. Add the onion and cook over a low heat until softened. Add the garlic and paprika and cook for 2 minutes. Add the peas, potatoes and peppers, along with the remaining olive oil. Turn the heat up and carefully stir until the ingredients are all evenly spread out.

Beat the eggs with the saffron and season with salt and pepper. Pour the egg mixture into the pan with the onion, potatoes and peppers and gently move the contents of the pan around with a fork to distibute evenly. Cook over high heat for 1 minute, then turn the heat down to low. Once the frittata is firm around the edges, is set about half way through and golden underneath, transfer the pan to the grill/broiler and cook until top is set and golden.

herby chickpea pancakes with halloumi and roasted corn and red pepper salsa

Serve these tasty, gluten-free pancakes for a substantial weekend brunch or as a light lunch or supper. The crunchy salsa can be made ahead of time and is also great added to salads.

130 g/1 cup chickpea/gram flour
1 teaspoon salt
½ teaspoon ground cumin
¼ teaspoon turmeric
½ can chickpeas, drained, rinsed
    and crushed with a fork
240 ml/1 cup milk
1 egg
1 garlic clove, crushed
freshly grated zest and juice of
    1 lemon
a handful of chopped fresh herbs
    (coriander/cilantro, parsley or
    chives all work well)
1 teaspoon bicarbonate of
    soda/baking soda
250 g/9 oz. halloumi, sliced
1 tablespoon olive oil

**For the roasted corn and red
    pepper salsa**
2 sweet red (bell) peppers, halved
2 sweetcorn cobs
a handful of cherry tomatoes
3 tablespoons olive oil
½ red onion, finely diced
½–1 fresh red chilli/chile,
    finely diced
a handful of fresh coriander/cilantro,
    finely chopped
freshly squeezed juice of ½ a lime
1 teaspoon white wine vinegar
1 teaspoon granulated sugar
salt and freshly ground black pepper

Serves 6–8

Preheat the oven to 200°C (400°F) Gas 6.

To make the salsa, put the peppers in a roasting pan skin-side up, with the sweetcorn cobs and tomatoes. Sprinkle generously with salt and pepper and drizzle with 2 tablespoons olive oil. Roast in the top half of the preheated oven for 20–25 minutes until the skin of the peppers has shrivelled and the corn is golden. Reserve any juices left in the pan. Peel the skin off the peppers and remove the corn kernels from the cobs. Finely chop the peppers and break up the tomatoes with a fork, then put them in a bowl with the onion, chilli/chile and coriander/cilantro.

In a separate bowl, combine the lime juice, vinegar, sugar and remaining olive oil. Season with salt and pepper and stir until well combined. Pour over the vegetable mixture and stir.

To make the chickpea pancakes, put the chickpea/gram flour, salt and cumin and turmeric in a bowl. Stir in the crushed chickpeas.

In a separate bowl, combine the milk, egg, garlic and lemon juice and zest and beat well with a fork until well combined.

Make a well in the centre of the dry ingredients, pour in the milk mixture and stir from the centre until well combined. Add the chopped herbs, cover and set aside in the fridge for 20 minutes or until you are ready to cook the pancakes. Just before you make the pancakes, stir in the bicarbonate of soda/baking soda.

Lightly grease a frying pan/skillet and set over medium–high heat. Add a ladle of batter and cook until bubbles begin to form and the pancake starts to firm up. Turn it over and cook until both sides are golden brown and it has puffed up slightly. You can keep the pancakes warm in a low oven until ready to serve.

Lightly oil the halloumi and cook over high heat on a stovetop griddle/grill pan for 1 minute on each side until golden. Put the pancakes onto serving plates, top with the salsa and serve.

granola with berry compote

Making your own granola is a great way to control what is going in to your breakfast cereal. It is easy to do and you can make a large batch and store it in an airtight container so that you can have homemade breakfast every day. Feel free to use any combination of dried fruit and nuts that you have to hand.

500 g/5 cups rolled oats
150 g/1⅓ cups mixed chopped nuts
150 g/1¼ cups mixed seeds
50 g dessicated/shredded coconut (optional)
½ teaspoon salt (optional)
2 teaspoons mixed/apple pie spice
2 eating apples, grated with skin on
2 tablespoons dark brown sugar
4 tablespoons vegetable, sunflower, canola or hazelnut oil
8 tablespoons runny honey, maple syrup or golden/light corn syrup
150 g/1 cup choppped mixed dried fruit of your choice
plain yogurt, to serve

For the berry compote
300 g/3 cups blackberries, blueberries and raspberries (fresh or frozen)
6 tablespoons honey or golden/light corn syrup
1–2 tablespoons brown sugar
freshly grated zest of 1 lemon
freshly squeezed juice of ½ a lemon
1 cinnamon stick or ½ teaspoon ground cinnamon (optional)
1 teaspoon vanilla extract

Makes 8 servings

Preheat the oven to 150°C (300°F) Gas 2.

Put the oats, nuts, seeds, coconut, salt and mixed/apple pie spice in a large mixing bowl, add the apple and stir until well combined.

Put the sugar, oil and honey in a saucepan set over low heat and stir until melted. Pour over the dry ingredients and stir until the mixture is well combined.

Spread the mixture evenly on the largest baking sheet you have, taking care not to heap the mixture to ensure that it cooks evenly. Bake in the preheated oven for 40–45 minutes, stirring every 10 minutes, until the granola is golden. Then add the dried fruit and bake for a further 5 minutes. If you can, watch the mixture quite closely in the oven to make sure that it does not burn.

To make the berry compote, put all the ingredients in a saucepan and set over low–medium heat. Simmer gently until the fruit has softened but is still holding its shape and the liquid has reduced. Turn off the heat and leave to cool.

Allow the granola to cool and then store it in an airtight container until ready to eat. Serve with a large spoonful each of plain yogurt and berry compote.

french toast stuffed with bananas

French toast is the perfect indulgence for a lazy Sunday morning, and it is especially good oozing with this delicious banana and nut filling. The berry compote adds a refreshingly fruity flavour but maple syrup is also good.

4 eggs
100 ml/scant 1 cup milk
1 banana
freshly grated zest and freshly
    squeezed juice of 1 orange
30 g/¼ cup almonds, pecans or
    walnuts, roughly chopped
    (optional)
½ teaspoon ground allspice
4 slices of white bread (slightly
    stale/dry or very lightly toasted
    in the oven)
15 g/1 tablespoon butter
salt and freshly ground black pepper

To serve
icing/confectioners' sugar (optional)
Berry Compote (page 22) or maple
    syrup, as preferred

Serves 2

Preheat the oven to 200°C (400°F) Gas 6.

Lightly beat the eggs, milk, and a little salt and pepper together in a small bowl. In a separate bowl, lightly crush the banana, then stir through the orange juice and zest, chopped nuts and allspice.

Spread the banana filling on 2 of the slices of bread, then top each with another slice of the bread to make 2 sandwiches. Soak the sandwiches in the egg mixture for 5–10 minutes, turning half way to make sure that both sides have absorbed the mixture.

Melt the butter in a frying pan/skillet set over medium heat, put the sandwiches into the pan and cook until brown on both sides. Finish them in the preheated oven for 5–10 minutes to heat through to the centre. Remove the sandwiches from the oven and slice on the diagonal. Dust liberally with icing/confectioners' sugar and serve with a spoonful of berry compote or maple syrup, as preferred.

honey and apricot breakfast muffins

These muffins are a fantastic grab-and-go midweek breakfast and contain lots of fruit, nuts and fibre to keep your energy levels high all morning. They also make the kitchen smell wonderful as they bake!

200 g/1½ cups plain/all-purpose flour
½ teaspoon bicarbonate of soda/baking soda
2½ teaspoons baking powder
2 teaspoons mixed/apple pie spice
50 g/½ cup chopped dried apricots
50 g/½ cup pecan nuts, chopped
100 g/1 cup porridge oats
50 g/½ cup sultanas/golden raisins
2 bananas (preferably soft)
2 unpeeled apples, grated
2 eggs
5 tablespoons vegetable oil
1 teaspoon vanilla extract
4 tablespoons honey
6 tablespoons milk
100 g/½ cup light brown sugar

a 12-hole muffin pan, lined with muffin cases

Makes 12

Preheat the oven to 180°C (350°F) Gas 4.

Sift the flour into a mixing bowl. Add the bicarbonate of soda/baking soda, baking powder and mixed/apple pie spice and stir to combine. Add the dried apricots, pecans and oats to the flour mixture together with the sultanas/golden raisins and set aside.

In a separate bowl, mash the bananas with a fork. Add the apples, eggs, oil, vanilla extract, honey and milk and stir to combine. Add the sugar and stir again.

Make a well in the centre of the dry ingredients. Pour in the wet ingredients and gently stir from the centre, gradually drawing in the dry ingredients to make a smooth batter.

Fill the muffin cases two thirds full and top with chopped pecans for added texture. Bake in the top half of the preheated oven for approximately 30–40 minutes until the muffins are well risen, golden and springy to touch. Remove from the oven and cool on a wire rack then serve with cups of hot coffee. These muffins are best eaten fresh but will keep in an airtight container for 3 or 4 days.

small bites

These recipes offer a sociable solution to food for friends, as they can be used as an indulgent snack, to start a meal or as a selection to be shared and enjoyed as you would a tapas or meze. From simply roasted figs and topped bruschetta, to crispy tempura and spicy samosas, use these dishes to mix and match and create your own culinary journey.

corncakes with spicy avocado salsa

These light, fresh-tasting corncakes are ideal served as a canapé with drinks. They also make a great brunch dish — simply make the corncakes slightly bigger (a tablespoon of batter makes a 6 cm/2½-inch-wide pancake), layer with the salsa and serve with a dollop of Sweet Chilli Jam (page 66).

225 g/1½ cups plus 1 tablespoon
   plain/all-purpose flour
1½ teaspoons baking powder
½ teaspoon salt
30 g/2 tablespoons butter
225 ml/1 cup milk
1 egg, lightly beaten
160 g/1 heaped cup canned or
   frozen sweetcorn
½–1 fresh red chilli/chile, finely
   chopped or 1 teaspoon chilli/hot
   red pepper flakes
a small handful of fresh coriander/
   cilantro, finely chopped
crème fraîche or sour cream,
   to serve

For the spicy avocado salsa
2 avocados, pitted
2 tablespoons freshly chopped
   coriander/cilantro, chopped
   (reserve a few leaves to garnish)
2 small shallots, finely chopped
1–2 fresh red chillis/chiles
   (depending how hot you want it!),
   finely chopped
freshly grated zest of 2 limes
2 tablespoons freshly squeezed
   lime juice
a pinch of sugar
salt and freshly ground black pepper

Makes 24

To make the spicy avocado salsa, half chop, half mash the avocado (depending on its ripeness) and with the herbs and shallots combine in a bowl, then add the remaining ingredients. Season well with salt and pepper. Taste and adjust the seasoning as required using more lime juice, chilli/chile or sugar, if needed.

For the corncakes, sift the flour into a mixing bowl and add the baking powder and salt. Set aside.

Melt the butter in a small saucepan set over low heat. In a separate bowl combine the milk, egg, sweetcorn, chilli/chile and coriander/cilantro. Add the melted butter and stir to combine.

Make a well in the centre of the dry ingredients. Pour in the wet ingredients and stir from the centre to gradually mix them together so that there are no lumps. Set aside for 10 minutes.

Lightly grease a frying pan/skillet and let it heat up over a medium-high heat. Put teaspoons of the mixture into the pan (it will spread a little). Cook until the pancakes are golden brown, turning over halfway through.

To serve, top with a spoonful of spicy avocado salsa, a little crème fraîche and a coriander/cilantro leaf.

lemon and mushroom risotto balls

Arancini (Sicilian stuffed rice balls) are a great way to serve risotto. They make a satisfying bite-size nibble, or 2 larger ones can be served as a starter.

30 g/2 tablespoons butter or
   olive oil
1 onion, grated or finely chopped
150 g/2½ cups finely chopped
   chestnut mushrooms
15 g/½ oz. dried porcini mushrooms,
   soaked in hot water until soft, and
   then finely chopped, reserving the
   soaking liquid (optional)
1 garlic clove, crushed
grated zest of 1 lemon and freshly
   squeezed juice from
   ½ a lemon
100 g/½ cup risotto rice
150 ml/⅔ cup dry white wine
   (optional)
300 ml/1¼ cups of vegetable stock
a small bunch of fresh parsley
50 g/⅔ cup grated Parmesan cheese
5 mm/¼-inch cubes red bell pepper
   (you could also use a few peas or
   diced courgette/zucchini per ball)
500 ml/about 2 cups vegetable oil
   for frying
salt and freshly ground black pepper
fresh mayonnaise, to serve
   (optional)

For the breadcrumb coating
50 g/⅓ cup plus 1 tablespoon
   plain/all-purpose flour, seasoned
   with salt and pepper
1 egg, lightly beaten
100 g/1¼ cups dried white
   breadcrumbs

Makes 16 small, or 8 large

To make the risotto, melt the butter in a heavy-based saucepan set over low heat. Add the onion and cook gently for about 10 minutes, then add the mushrooms and cook until softened. Add the garlic and cook for another minute.

Turn up the heat to medium and add the lemon zest and rice. Stir well and until the rice becomes opaque. Add the white wine, if using, and stir until all the liquid has been absorbed. Add about 200 ml/¾ cup of the stock and stir until the liquid is absorbed. Add any leftover liquid from the porcini mushrooms, being careful not to add any sediment. Stir well until the liquid has been absorbed, then keep adding stock and stirring until the risotto rice is cooked (about 20 minutes) – the rice will have softened but still have a slight bite. Make sure the liquid is well evaporated — the consistency should be thicker than a normal risotto so that the risotto balls will hold their shape. Remember that the rice mixture will thicken slightly when cooled. While the risotto is still hot, stir the Parmesan and parsley through it until incorporated.

Spread the rice on a large plate or tray to cool it quickly to room temperature, then form it into bite-size balls (about 40 g/1½ oz. each). To fill the balls, put each one in the palm of your hand and push down into the centre with your thumb, and put a few red pepper cubes in, then cover with the rice and roll back into a ball.

For the breadcrumb coating, place the flour, lightly beaten egg and breadcrumbs in 3 separate bowls. Roll each ball in the flour and tap off any excess. Then roll in egg and then in the breadcrumbs. For an extra crunchy coating, repeat the breadcrumb coating. Set the balls aside in the fridge until you are ready to fry.

Pour the vegetable oil into a deep stainless steel pan, filling it no more than halfway. Taking care, heat the oil to 160°C/325°F (if you do not have a thermometer, the oil is at the correct temperature when a small piece of bread dropped into it takes 60 seconds to turn golden brown). If the oil is too hot, the outer crumb coating might burn before the centre is cooked. Cook no more than 4 balls at a time until golden brown (1–2 minutes). Drain excess oil on paper towels, and serve warm with mayonnaise, if liked.

courgette fritters with minted yogurt

These fritters are perfect for enjoying with drinks. We like them made with courgettes but you can use carrots, beetroot or onions, if preferred. You can add feta, herbs, spices and chilli for extra flavour – just experiment with whatever you find in your fridge.

250 g/3 cups grated courgette/
    zucchini
4 spring onions/scallions,
    finely sliced
grated zest and freshly squeezed
    juice of 1 lemon
1 teaspoon vegetable oil, plus extra
    for deep-frying
3 tablespoons gram/chickpea flour
1 teaspoon baking powder
sea salt

For the minted yogurt
½ English cucumber, deseeded
    and grated
200 g/1 cup thick plain yogurt
½ garlic clove, crushed
a handful of fresh mint, chopped
a squeeze of fresh lemon juice
½ teaspoon sugar
salt and freshly ground black pepper

Makes 4 servings

To make the minted yogurt dip, put the grated cucumber in a strainer set over a bowl and leave for 10 minutes to drain any excess liquid. Alternatively you can squeeze out any liquid in a clean kitchen towel. Put the drained grated cucumber in a bowl with the yogurt. Add and stir in the crushed garlic and the chopped mint. Add a squeeze of lemon juice, sugar and season well with salt and pepper. Taste and adjust the seasoning with more lemon juice, sugar or salt if necessary.

To make the fritters, sprinkle the courgette/zucchini with salt and put it in a strainer set over a bowl for 10 minutes to draw out any moisture. Rinse the courgette/zucchini well with water to remove the salt, then squeeze out any excess liquid using a clean kitchen towel. Put the drained grated courgette/zucchini in a bowl, add the spring onions/scallions, lemon zest and juice and teaspoon of vegetable oil, and stir till thoroughly mixed. Combine the gram flour and baking powder, sprinkle them over the vegetables, then stir until well combined.

These fritters are best made in a deep-fat fryer. If you don't have a deep-fat fryer, put about 2 cm/¾ inch of oil in the bottom of a wok. Heat the oil until it is 180°C/350°F – hot but not smoking. (If you do not have a thermometer, the oil is at the correct temperature when a small piece of bread dropped into it takes 40 seconds to turn golden brown.)

Remove the fritters with a slotted spoon and drain on paper towels. Sprinkle the fritters with sea salt while they are still hot. The fritters are best served immediately but will keep for a short time in a warm oven.

vegetable dumplings with dipping sauce

These tasty dumplings make a good sharing plate or appetizer — they can be made ahead of time and frozen. Buy the wrappers from your local Asian store or order them online and use whatever you have in the fridge for the filling. Pour the delicious dipping sauce over some grated carrot for a quick salad or salsa.

1 tablespoon sesame oil
120 g/4 oz. Shitake mushrooms
1 pak choi/bok choy
1 carrot, grated
6 spring onions/scallions, finely sliced
2 garlic cloves
1–2 fresh red chillis/chiles
2-cm/¾-inch piece of fresh ginger, grated
a handful of fresh coriander/cilantro
1 pack of frozen round dumpling (gyoza) wrappers or wonton wrappers, defrosted
cornflour/cornstarch for dusting
sesame oil for frying (optional)

For the dipping sauce
3 tablespoons dark soy sauce or tamari
2 teaspoons dark brown sugar
1 tablespoon sesame oil
2 tablespoons rice vinegar (or white wine vinegar if you don't have it)
1 garlic clove, crushed
1 teaspoon finely grated fresh ginger
½–1 fresh red chilli/chile, very finely chopped
a squeeze of fresh lemon juice
a handful of fresh coriander/cilantro, chopped

a bamboo — or other — steamer, lined with parchment paper

Makes 18

(V)

To make the dipping sauce, put all of the ingredients in a small bowl and stir until well combined.

To make the dumplings, heat the sesame oil in a frying pan/skillet set over medium–high heat and add the mushrooms, pak choi/bok choy and carrot. Cook for about 5 minutes, until softened. Put the cooked mushrooms, pak choi/bok choy and carrots in a food processor along with the spring onions/scallions, garlic, chilli, ginger and coriander/cilantro and blitz. Alternatively, finely chop all of the ingredients by hand.

Dust the work surface with a little cornflour/cornstarch and put the dumpling wrappers on the floured surface. Put 1 teaspoon of the filling in the centre of each wrapper. Using a pastry brush, moisten the edges of each wrapper with a little water, then seal the edges together starting at the centre and ensuring there is no air trapped in the wrapper. Make sure that the dumpling is well sealed — if not, add a little more water to seal it. You can use your finger to frill the edge of the dumpling for decoration.

Put the bamboo steamer over a pan of boiling water. If you do not have a steamer, cover a colander with a make-shift kitchen foil lid. Put the dumplings in the parchment-lined steamer, cover with a lid and steam for 10–15 minutes until the filling is hot and cooked.

For extra flavour and texture, once the dumplings have been steamed, heat a tablespoon of sesame oil in a frying pan over a high heat and fry the dumplings for 1–2 minutes, until the bottom and sides start to colour. Be careful as they colour quickly and can easily burn.

The uncooked dumplings will keep covered in the fridge for a few hours. Alternatively, steam the dumplings, let them cool, then store them, well wrapped, in the fridge for a few hours. Resteam until they are hot again.

chicory leaves stuffed with beetroot, cumin and mixed grains

This tasty and colourful salad makes a great addition to any buffet. The chicory leaf gives a bitter edge to cut through the sweetness of the beetroot. It's a good dish to prepare in advance, but hold back some herbs and pistachios to sprinkle on top, as the beetroot colours everything.

50 g/heaped ¼ cup basmati rice
5 cardamon pods
50 g/heaped ¼ cup quinoa
2 teaspoons cumin seeds
2 teaspoons fennel seeds
100 g/¾ cup canned chickpeas*, strained and rinsed well
grated zest and freshly squeezed juice of 2 limes
a small handful of fresh coriander/ cilantro leaves, finely chopped, plus extra to serve
½ raw beetroot/beet, peeled and grated (gloves are advisable as beetroot dyes your hands)
70 g/½ cup pistachios, whole or roughly chopped, plus extra to serve
2 tablespoons groundnut/peanut oil (or olive oil, rapeseed/canola oil all work well)
a pinch of sugar
15 middle-outer chicory/Belgian endive leaves, washed and dried
salt and freshly ground black pepper

Makes 15

Wash the rice well and put it in a large saucepan with boiling salted water and the cardamon pods. Cook according to the packet instructions until soft but still with a bite. Strain well, spread on a tray to cool down and set aside.

Meanwhile, cook the quinoa in boiling salted water — just enough to cover the grains by 5 mm/¼ inch. Gently simmer for about 10 minutes, until softened but retaining a bite. Strain well, spread on a tray to cool down and set aside.

Lightly toast the cumin and fennel seeds in a dry frying pan/skillet set over medium heat — just until you can smell the aromas of the seeds releasing — then turn off the heat, remove from the pan and set aside.

In a bowl, combine the chickpeas, rice, quinoa, lime zest, coriander/cilantro, cumin and fennel seeds, beetroot/beet, pistachios, salt and pepper, and mix well.

Taste the mixture and season with the oil, lime juice, sugar, salt and pepper. Once seasoned, fill the chicory/endive leaves generously and sprinkle with coriander/cilantro and the remaining pistachios.

*Note: if using dried chickpeas, these will need to be soaked overnight and cooked in simmering water for about 15 minutes before use.

samosas with lemon and garlic yogurt dip

Samosas are easier to make than they look. Traditionally deep-fried, they can also be baked, as here. We've given you two delicious recipes for fillings, so choose your favourite or make both! Each quantity of filling will be sufficient to fill 18 samosas.

100 g/½ cup minus 1 tablespoon
    butter
1 packet (12 sheets) of filo/phyllo
    pastry dough
2 tablespoons poppy seeds or
    sesame seeds (optional)

For the butternut squash filling
1 butternut squash (400 g/14 oz.),
    peeled and cut into chunks
2 tablespoons olive oil
300 g/11 oz. spinach
2 garlic cloves, crushed
1½ teaspoons ground cumin
1 teaspoon ground coriander
2 tablespoons chopped fresh
    flat-leaf parsley
finely grated zest from 1 lemon
50 g/⅓ cup pine nuts (optional)
salt and freshly ground black pepper

For the courgette/zucchini filling
2 courgettes/zucchini, deseeded
120 g/1 cup sundried tomatoes
200 g/7 oz. feta
finely grated zest of 1 lemon
1 garlic clove, crushed
½ teaspoon chilli/red pepper flakes
1 teaspoon mustard seeds
¼ nutmeg, grated
salt and freshly ground black pepper

For the lemon and garlic yogurt dip
300 ml/about 1½ cups plain yogurt
grated zest and juice of 2 lemons
2 garlic cloves, crushed
salt and freshly ground black pepper

Makes 18

Preheat the oven to 190°C (375°F) Gas 5.

To make the butternut squash filling, toss the chopped butternut with the oil, put on a baking sheet and bake in the oven for 20–30 minutes until soft but still holding its shape. Remove from the oven and set aside to cool. Meanwhile, wilt the spinach in a sauté pan set over low heat with the lid on. Once wilted, squeeze excess water out of the spinach and set aside to cool. Put the garlic, ground cumin and coriander, parsley, lemon zest and pine nuts (if using) in a bowl, and once cool, add the spinach and butternut squash. Season to taste with salt and pepper, and set aside.

To make the courgette/zucchini filling, cube the courgette/zucchini and remove excess liquid following the instructions given on page 35. Chop the sundried tomatoes and feta put in a bowl with the lemon zest, garlic, chilli/hot red pepper flakes, mustard seeds and nutmeg. Combine well and season to taste with salt and pepper. Set aside until ready to fill samosas.

To make the yogurt dip, combine the yogurt, lemon zest and garlic in a bowl; season to taste with lemon juice, salt and pepper.

Preheat oven to 200°C (400°F) Gas 6.

To make the samosas, melt the butter in a small saucepan set over low heat. Brush one sheet of pastry dough with melted butter, then lay another pastry sheet on top (giving you 2 layers of filo). Cut each layered sheet into 3 strips. Lightly brush with butter. (Keep the remaining pastry well covered under a damp kitchen towel until needed.) Put a tablespoon of filling at one end of a strip leaving a 1-cm/⅜-inch gap at the bottom and on either side. Form the filling into a rough triangle, and fold the bottom excess up onto the filling. Roll the samosa up tightly, making the shape of the triangle. Brush with butter and sprinkle with poppy or sesame seeds, and put on a lined baking sheet. Repeat with the remaining pastry.

Bake in the oven for 10–12 minutes until the samosas are golden brown, and serve immediately, with lemon and garlic yogurt dip.

vegetable tempura with wasabi dipping sauce

This is our take on a Japanese classic, which is quick and simple. Great as a nibble or appetizer, serve with a dipping sauce, soy sauce, sweet chilli sauce or simply a squeeze of lemon juice. Tempura gives the traditional crudités a modern twist, and a more interesting texture for just a little extra effort.

1 large courgette/zucchini, core removed and discarded, flesh cut into 1- x 5-cm/³⁄₈- x 2-inch strips
1 large aubergine/eggplant, cut into rings
500 ml/about 2 cups vegetable oil, for frying
40 g/¹⁄₃ cup plain/all-purpose flour
60 g/¹⁄₂ cup plus 1¹⁄₂ tablespoons cornflour/cornstarch
¹⁄₄ teaspoon baking powder
100–150 ml/¹⁄₃–²⁄₃ cup iced sparkling water
a pinch of salt
¹⁄₂ head of cauliflower, cut into bite-size florets
¹⁄₂ head of broccoli, cut into bite-size florets
3 red bell peppers, deseeded and cut into strips

For the wasabi dipping sauce
2 teaspoons wasabi powder
2 tablespoons sesame oil
zest and freshly squeezed juice of 1 lime
1 fresh red chilli/chile, finely chopped
2 tablespoons soy sauce
3 cm/1¹⁄₄ inch piece of fresh ginger, peeled and grated
a pinch of sugar or 1 teaspoon maple syrup

Makes 4–6 servings

For best results, place the courgette/zucchini and aubergine/eggplant in a sieve/strainer and sprinkle all over with table salt, then leave for 10 minutes; you will notice liquid has leached out of the vegetables. Rinse well in water to remove the salt and pat dry.

To make the wasabi dipping sauce, put the wasabi powder in a bowl and gradually add the sesame oil to form a smooth paste. Slowly add the lime zest and juice, and the chilli/chile, soy sauce, ginger and sugar, while continually stirring to thoroughly combine. Taste, and alter seasoning if necessary.

Set your deep-fat fryer to 190°C (375°F), or fill a wide deep saucepan ¹⁄₃ full with vegetable oil and set over medium heat. The oil is at the correct temperature when a small piece of bread dropped into it takes 20 seconds to turn golden brown.

Make the batter immediately before cooking. Combine the flour, cornflour/cornstarch and baking powder in a bowl. Add the water to the flour mixture, whisking to combine quickly, but stop as soon as the liquid is combined — the odd lump is ok, and better than over-working the batter. The consistency should be slightly looser than a crêpe batter — a light coating batter is what you want, not one that is thick and gloopy. The batter also must be ice cold, so drop an ice cube in the batter to keep it chilled while using.

As soon as the oil has come to temperature (see page 32), make sure the vegetables are dry and then dip them in the batter, shake off any excess and put them into the hot oil using a slotted metal spoon. Cook for 1–2 minutes until pale golden (tempura does not colour like other batter so do not wait for a deep colour). Repeat, cooking in small batches as cooking too much at the same time can reduce the oil temperature. When cooked, put the tempura on paper towels to drain and lightly sprinkle with salt. Serve immediately with wasabi dipping sauce or a squeeze of lemon.

breadcrumbed halloumi goujons

Served warm and oozing with melted halloumi cheese, these breadcrumbed bites are hard to resist! To add a little heat, you can either serve with Spicy Tomato Ketchup, or add a pinch of hot smoked paprika to the breadcrumbs.

50 g/⅓ cup plus 1 tablespoon plain/all-purpose flour, seasoned with salt and pepper

1 egg, lightly beaten

150 g/2 cups dried white breadcrumbs

a pinch of smoked hot paprika (optional)

250 g/9 oz. halloumi, cut into 8 slices

500 ml/about 2 cups vegetable oil, for frying

salt and freshly ground black pepper

lemon wedges, to serve

Spicy Tomato Ketchup (page 64), to serve (optional)

Makes 8

For the breadcrumb coating, put the flour, egg and breadcrumbs in 3 separate bowls. Take the slices of halloumi and coat them in flour, tapping off any excess. Next coat them in the egg and finally the breadcrumbs. For an extra crunchy coating repeat the process.

If you have a deep-fat fryer, set the temperature to 160°C (325°F); if not, pour the vegetable oil into a deep stainless steel pan and fill no more than half-full with oil. To test the temperature of the oil, drop a small piece of bread in the pan — it should take 60 seconds to turn golden brown.

Put the breadcrumbed halloumi into the hot oil and fry until golden brown (this will take 3–4 minutes). Dry off the halloumi on paper towels and sprinkle with sea salt. Serve warm with lemon wedges for squeezing or Spicy Tomato Ketchup for dipping, if liked.

mini bruschettas

Bruschettas are a classic Italian antipasti. Having a few quick recipes for bruschetta toppings up your sleeve means you can whip up a platter of delicious, fresh-tasting bites with the minimum of effort.

1 ciabatta or baguette, sliced and lightly toasted or grilled
olive oil, for drizzling
fresh flat-leaf parsley, chopped
salt and freshly ground black pepper

For the olive and caper topping
500g/4 cups pitted black olives, finely chopped
2 garlic cloves, crushed
4 tablespoons capers, well rinsed
grated zest and juice of 2 lemons
1 teaspoon chilli/hot red pepper flakes
a pinch of sugar
a splash of extra virgin olive oil
4 tablespoons/¼ cup of fresh flat-leaf parsley, finely chopped

For the roasted tomato and pepper topping
2 red bell peppers, deseeded
400 g/14 oz. fresh plum tomatoes
2 garlic cloves, whole and unpeeled
6 tablespoons olive oil

For the fresh herb pesto topping
2 large handfuls fresh flat-leaf parsley leave
1 large handful fresh basil leaves
2 garlic cloves, crushed
grated zest and juice of 2 lemons
40 g/⅔ cup grated Parmesan (optional)
100 g/¾ cup pine nuts, lightly toasted and chopped
6 tablespoons extra virgin olive oil

Each recipe makes sufficient topping for 16 small toasts

To make the olive and caper topping, whizz the olives, garlic, capers, lemon zest, chilli/hot red pepper flakes, sugar, olive oil and parsley in a blender. Vary the texture according to your preference: it can either be slightly chunky with some pieces of olive for a bit of bite, or puréed. Season to taste with lemon juice, salt, pepper and an extra pinch of sugar if the olives have a particularly sour edge. Don't add salt before tasting, as olives are usually salty enough already.

For the roasted tomato and pepper topping, preheat the oven to 200°C (400°F) Gas 6.

Halve the bell peppers and put them with the tomatoes, and garlic on a baking sheet lined with foil, sprinkle with salt and drizzle with olive oil, and put in the oven. Remove the garlic when soft (after 10–15 minutes) and set aside. Remove the tomatoes after 20–25 minutes and set aside. Remove the peppers after 30 minutes, when their skins have coloured, and put them in a sealed plastic bag (this steams the peppers so their skins are easily removed). Once the tomatoes are cool, remove and discard the skins and put the flesh in a bowl. Squeeze the garlic cloves out of their skins into the same bowl. Once the peppers are cool, remove from the plastic bag and peel away their skins. Roughly chop the peppers and tomatoes and put them back in the bowl. Mix to combine well and season to taste with salt and pepper.

For the fresh herb pesto topping, combine all the ingredients in a bowl and add half the lemon juice. Lightly pulse in a small food blender to give a smooth finish and season to taste with salt, pepper and extra lemon juice if necessary.

Serve the assorted toppings on lightly toasted or grilled ciabatta slices, finish with a small drizzle of extra virgin olive oil and chopped flat-leaf parsley. Assemble just before you are ready to serve, otherwise the bread will become soggy.

roasted figs with sweet sherry dressing

These roasted figs are a really quick and versatile dish. Serve them as a light appetizer or as a sharing plate with mozzarella, rocket and pine nuts. You can even use a sweeter sherry and add a half-teaspoon of vanilla extract and serve them with some extra honey and vanilla ice cream for dessert.

30 g/2 tablespoons butter
2 tablespoons runny honey,
    maple syrup or agave nectar
4 tablespoons/¼ cup medium dry
    sherry (such as amontillado
    sherry)
8 fresh figs
2 balls of fresh buffalo mozzarella
    (optional)
several large handfuls of wild
    rocket/arugula
50 g/¼ cup toasted pine nuts

Serves 4

Preheat the oven to 180°C (350°F) Gas 4.

Put the butter, honey and sherry in a small saucepan and set over a low heat. Heat gently until the butter has melted and the ingredients are well combined and syrupy.

Using a sharp knife, cut a cross through the top of the figs, almost to the base. Gently push in at the base of the figs so that they open out at the top like a flower and put them in a buttered baking dish. Pour the sherry mixture over the figs and bake in the preheated oven for about 15 minutes until the figs are soft.

Put the figs on a serving dish. Tear the mozzarella into pieces and put a few in each fig. Surround with rocket/arugula and scatter over some toasted pine nuts. Pour the juices from the baking dish the top and serve immediately.

dips, salsas and sauces

These quick and delicious recipes will bring the simplest of vegetarian dishes to life. Add freshness and colour with beetroot remoulade, depth of flavour with seasonal pestos, or sweetness and spice with our chilli jam and spicy tomato ketchup.

beetroot, celeriac and apple remoulade

This deliciously crunchy remoulade makes the perfect side dish to any savoury quiche or tart. It's also ideal for a light lunch or as a snack, shown here served with creamy goat cheese toasts.

grated zest and juice of 1 lemon
5 tablespoons/⅓ cup fresh
  mayonnaise (you can use the
  recipe on page 19, omitting the
  garlic, or use storebought)
2 apples, skin on, grated
¼ celeriac/celery root, peeled
  and grated
1 garlic clove, crushed
2 teaspoons fresh dill, finely
  chopped, plus a few extra sprigs,
  to serve
2 teaspoons Dijon mustard
1 teaspoon horseradish cream
2 small raw beetroots/beets, peeled
  and grated
a handful of chopped walnuts
  (optional)
salt and freshly ground black pepper

Goat cheese toasts (optional)
1 crusty baguette
100 g/3½ oz. goat cheese
a drizzle of olive oil

Serves 4–6

To make the remoulade, put the lemon zest and the juice in a small bowl with the mayonnaise. Add the remaining lemon juice to a bowl of cold water and put the apple and celeriac/celery root in the water so that it does not discolour.

Add the garlic, dill, mustard and horseradish cream to the mayonnaise and season to taste with salt and pepper. Drain the celeriac/celery root and apple and stir it through the mayonnaise mixture, together with the grated beetroot/beets.

To make the goat cheese toasts, preheat the grill/broiler to hot. Cut the baguette into slices on an angle, spread one side with the goat cheese, then drizzle with olive oil. Toast under the grill/broiler until warm and golden.

Spoon the remoulade into a serving bowl, scatter over it some chopped walnuts and sprigs of dill and serve with the warm goat cheese toasts on the side.

sweet potato hummus with breadsticks

This velvety smooth sweet potato hummus dip makes an interesting change from the more familiar chickpea version. The breadsticks are simple to make and their crunchy texture makes them the perfect accompaniment here. Those on a gluten-free diet can enjoy the dip with root vegetable crisps/chips.

1 sweet potato, unpeeled
3 garlic cloves, unpeeled
½ x 400-g/14-oz. can of chickpeas
1 fresh red chilli/chile, finely chopped
a handful of fresh coriander/cilantro leaves, chopped
2 tablespoons olive oil
grated zest and freshly squeezed juice of ½ a lime
salt and freshly ground black pepper

For the breadsticks (optional)
300 g/2¼ cups plain/all-purpose flour
2 teaspoons fast-action yeast
2 teaspoons salt
1 teaspoon sugar
120–150 ml/½–⅔ cup lukewarm water
4 tablespoons/¼ cup olive oil
a pinch of mixed dried herbs, a pinch of cayenne pepper or salt and freshly ground black pepper

Serves 4–6

To make the sweet potato hummus, preheat the oven to 180°C (350°F) Gas 4.

Roast the sweet potato in a roasting pan for 30–40 minutes until very soft. Add the garlic cloves to the pan about 20 minutes before the end of the cooking time.

Remove from the oven and, when cool enough to handle, remove and discard the skins from the sweet potato and garlic cloves. Put the chickpeas, chilli/chile, coriander/cilantro, olive oil and lime zest in a food processor and blitz until they reach the desired consistency. Season with salt, pepper and lime juice to taste.

To make the breadsticks, preheat the oven to 170°C (340°F) Gas 4. Combine the flour, yeast, salt and sugar in a bowl. Make a well in the centre, pour in the olive oil and water, and stir until well combined and the dough comes together. It should be soft but not sticky.

Knead the dough for about 10 minutes by hand, cover with oiled clingfilm/plastic wrap or a damp cloth and leave it to rise in a warm place for 40 minutes – 1 hour, or until doubled in size.

Divide the dough in half and keep half wrapped up so that it does not dry out. Roll half the dough out into a flat rectangle about 0.5–1 cm/¼–⅜-inch thick, then cut it into 1-cm/⅜-inch-wide strips. Roll the strips into pencil-width tubes. Repeat with the other half of the dough. Spread the mixed dried herbs, cayenne pepper or salt and pepper on a board, then roll the breadsticks in them and put them on a floured baking sheet. Bake in the preheated oven for 20–30 minutes until golden. Cool on a wire rack.

When ready to serve, spoon the sweet potato hummus into a serving bowl and serve with the cooled breadsticks on the side for dipping.

roasted aubergine and red onion dip with paprika pitta crisps

This rich and earthy dip is very similar to the popular Middle Eastern dish baba ganoush. It can be made the day before, and is easily adapted to include other spices such as cumin, fennel or chilli. You can also bake the pittas in cayenne pepper, sumac or five-spice powder for a slightly different flavour.

1 large aubergine/eggplant
2 red onions, quartered
4 garlic cloves, left whole
grated zest and freshly squeezed
    juice of 1 lemon
a pinch of sugar
4 tablespoons/¼ cup olive oil
salt and freshly ground black pepper

**For the paprika pitta crisps
    (optional)**
5 pitta breads, halved lengthways
    and cut into strips
1 tablespoon paprika (plain
    or smoked)
2 tablespoons olive oil

To serve
2 tablespoons pomegranate seeds
    (optional)
1 tablespoon extra virgin olive oil,
    for drizzling

Serves 4–6

To make the roasted aubergine/eggplant and red onion dip, preheat the oven to 190°C (375°F) Gas 5.

Put the aubergine/eggplant, onions and garlic on a baking sheet and put them in the preheated oven. Bake for 40–45 minute until soft, but remove the garlic after 10–15 minutes and the onions after 20–25 minutes.

When cooked, cut the aubergine/eggplant in half, scoop out the flesh, and put it in a blender. Squeeze the garlic cloves out of their skins, remove and discard the soft cores and skins of the onions.

Blend the aubergine/eggplant, onions, garlic, lemon zest, sugar, olive oil, and salt and pepper to a purée. Taste and adjust the seasoning with lemon juice, sugar, salt and pepper, if needed.

To make the paprika pitta crisps, turn the oven up to 200°C (400°F) Gas 6. Drizzle a fresh baking sheet with the olive oil and then sprinkle with the paprika, salt and pepper. Put the pitta bread strips on the baking sheet and mix to coat. Bake in the oven for 8 minutes until slightly coloured and crisp.

Put the dip in a serving bowl and sprinkle with pomegranate seeds, if using. Drizzle with extra virgin olive oil and serve with the pitta crisps on the side for dipping.

four punchy pestos

Pestos make fantastic sauces for freshly cooked pasta but can also add colour and flavour to a wide variety of other dishes. Use them as you would a relish to spice up simple fritattas and quiches, serve them spread on crostini as attractive canapés, or spread them on fresh bread for a quick and tasty snack.

For the roasted beetroot pesto
1 large roasted beetroot/beet
1 tablespoon chopped dill
grated zest of ½ a lemon, freshly squeezed juice of 1
a handful of fresh flat leaf parsley leaves, chopped
a handful of wild rocket/arugula
1 garlic clove, crushed
2 tablespoons extra virgin olive oil
a handful of toasted walnuts
2 teaspoons capers
1 tablespoon cream cheese (optional)

For the ricotta and herb pesto
250 g/9 oz. ricotta
a large handful of fresh flat-leaf parsley leaves
a large handful of fresh mint leaves
grated zest of 1 lemon, freshly squeezed juice of 2
2 garlic cloves
2 fresh red chillies/chiles
salt and freshly ground black pepper
toasted pine nuts for sprinkling

Each recipe makes 4–6

servings

For the watercress pesto
a large handful of watercress (about 50 g/1 cup)
grated zest of 1 lemon, and freshly squeezed juice to taste
50 g/⅓ cup blanched almonds, toasted
6 tablespoons (⅓ cup plus 1 tablespoon) extra virgin olive oil
20 g/about ⅓ cup grated Parmesan
1 garlic clove, crushed
salt and freshly ground black pepper, to taste

For the mushroom and walnut pesto
320 g/4½–5½ cups chestnut mushrooms fried in 1 tablespoon olive oil
2 garlic cloves
2 tablespoons walnut oil
½ teaspoon dried rosemary
1 fresh red chilli/chile
freshly squeezed juice of ½ a lemon
a handful of chopped flat-leaf parsley leaves
a handful of walnuts

For each of the pestos, put all of the ingredients in a food processor and blitz until they form a loose paste. If you would like the mixture to be a bit looser, simply drizzle in some extra oil.

If you do not have a food processor, you can finely chop all of the ingredients and bash them together in a large mortar and pestle.

Although the pestos are best served when freshly made, they will keep for up to 3 days, when stored in an airtight container in the fridge.

caponata

In Italy caponata is enjoyed as a warm vegetable side dish or as part of a cold vegetable antipasto. Our take on this classic Sicilian recipe is best enjoyed at room temperature as a dip with toasted ciabatta. It keeps well so can be made ahead and enjoyed the next day.

1 aubergine/eggplant, cubed
1 teaspoon cinnamon
2 tablespoons olive oil
1 red onion, chopped
2 celery stalks, sliced
1 garlic clove, crushed
1 x 400-g/14-oz. can chopped
    tomatoes
a handful of sultanas/golden raisins
2 tablespoons white wine
2 teaspoons capers, drained
1 tablespoon white wine vinegar
2 teaspoons sugar
a squeeze of fresh lemon juice

To serve
a handful of chopped fresh flat-leaf
    parsley leaves
a drizzle of extra virgin olive oil
freshly squeezed lemon juice
slices of ciabatta, toasted

Serves 4—6

Season the aubergine/eggplant cubes generously with salt and pepper, and sprinkle with cinnamon. Heat the olive oil in a large frying pan/skillet set over low heat, add the aubergine/eggplant and cook for about 10 minutes until soft and starting to turn golden. Remove the aubergine/eggplant from the pan and set aside until needed.

Return the pan to the heat and add the onion, celery and garlic, and cook for about 8 minutes until the vegetables begin to soften. Add the tomatoes, sultanas/golden raisins and white wine, and simmer over low heat for about 20 minutes. Stir in the cooked aubergine/eggplant, add the capers, vinegar, sugar and lemon juice, and cook over low heat until the taste of vinegar softens. Remove from the heat and allow to cool to room temperature.

Stir in the parsley and add a drizzle of olive oil and a squeeze of lemon juice. Spoon onto slices of toasted ciabatta to serve.

quick fresh salsas

These versatile salsas take no time at all to prepare and can be used to liven up a wide variety of simply prepared foods.

Apple, celery and mint salsa

2 teaspoons white wine vinegar

1 teaspoon caster/superfine sugar

1 apple, skin on, cored and chopped

2 small celery stalks, sliced

3 spring onions/scallions,
   finely sliced

a handful of fresh mint leaves,
   chopped

a handful of walnuts, roughly
   chopped

salt and freshly ground black pepper

Makes 4–6 servings

(V)

Combine the vinegar and sugar in a bowl and season well with salt and pepper. Put the apple, celery, spring onions/scallions, mint and walnuts and in a separate bowl and stir the vinegar mixture through it. Season to taste with salt and pepper.

Carrot, orange and mint salsa

1 teaspoon grated ginger

grated zest of 1 lemon and a
   squeeze of lemon juice

2 tablespoons olive oil

3–4 teaspoons white wine vinegar

2 carrots, peeled and grated

2 oranges, peeled and cut into
   segments

a handful of fresh mint, chopped

a sprinkling of poppy seeds
   (optional)

salt and freshly ground
   black pepper

Makes 4–6 servings

(V)

Combine the ginger, lemon zest and juice, olive oil and vinegar in a small bowl and season well with salt and pepper. Put the carrots, oranges and mint in a separate bowl. Add the ginger and lemon mixture and toss to combine. Sprinkle with poppy seeds just before serving, if using.

Asian cucumber salsa

1 cucumber, cut into ribbons using
   a peeler

2½ teaspoons salt

1 tablespoon rice vinegar

2 teaspoons caster/superfine sugar

a sprinkling of sesame seeds

Makes 4–6 servings

Put the cucumber ribbons in a sieve/strainer set over a bowl, sprinkle with salt and leave for 5–10 minutes to allow the liquid to drain out. Rinse off the salt and squeeze out any moisture in a clean kitchen towel and put the cucumber in a bowl.

Mix the rice vinegar, sugar and ½ teaspoon salt in a separate bowl, pour it over the cucumber ribbons and toss to combine. If you would like the cucumber to be soft, let it marinate for a couple of hours. Sprinkle with sesame seeds just before serving.

spicy tomato ketchup

After making your own tomato ketchup you won't want to go back to the store-bought stuff! It is irresistable served with chunky, potato wedges or breadcrumbed halloumi (see page 44). It also makes a lovely gift for foodies.

2 tablespoons olive oil
2 red onions, finely chopped
1 celery stalk, finely sliced
4-cm/1½-inch piece of fresh ginger, grated
2 garlic cloves, crushed
2 teaspoons chilli/hot red pepper flakes
1½ tablespoons cumin seeds
1½ tablespoons fennel seeds
4 x 400-g/14-oz. cans chopped plum tomatoes
2 tablespoons red wine vinegar
2 tablespoons balsamic vinegar
1 teaspoon white sugar
2 tablespoons light brown sugar
2 tablespoons tomato purée/paste
2 teaspoons lemon thyme, chopped
2 bay leaves
salt and freshly ground black pepper

Makes 600 ml/about 2½ cups

Ⓥ

Heat the oil in a large deep pan over low heat, add the onions and 2 tablespoons of water, and cook gently until soft. If the onions start to stick to the bottom, add a little more water. Add the celery and cook until soft. Add the ginger, garlic and spices and let cook for 1 minute. Add the rest of the ingredients, bring to the boil and then reduce to a low simmer and cook, uncovered, for about 45 minutes to reduce and thicken. If the tomato mixture still looks quite thin, turn up the heat and continue to reduce until thick.

Remove from the heat and let cool slightly. Discard the bay leaves and blend the mixture using a hand/immersion blender. Season with salt and pepper and leave it as is for a slightly chunky version or, for a silky smooth version, push the mixture through a fine mesh sieve/strainer using the back of a ladle in circular motions.

To bottle and seal the ketchup, preheat the oven to 100°C (215°F) Gas ½. Wash the bottles with hot soapy water and bake in the oven for about 20 minutes. Pour the warm ketchup into the warm, sterilized bottles. Leave a small gap at the top of each bottle and seal immediately. If properly sterilized and sealed the ketchup should keep for a couple of months. Once open store in the fridge and consume within 3 weeks.

sweet chilli jam

This fiery jam is a really useful ingredient to have to hand and is so much better than storebought varieties. It is quite hot, but the sweetness tempers this beautifully. It will store for a long time, though it never lasts very long because it's just so good! Serve it with egg dishes, cheese or in sandwiches.

2–3 fresh red chillies/chiles,
    including the seeds*
6 garlic cloves
4-cm/1½-inch piece of fresh ginger
500 g/2½ cups white sugar
250 g/1¼ cups dark brown sugar
250 ml/1 cup red wine vinegar
1 kg/2¼ lbs. red, yellow and/or
    orange peppers, chopped
1 x 400-g/14-oz. can chopped
    tomatoes
2 teaspoons soy sauce (optional)

Makes 1 litre/about 4 cups

*This recipe makes a medium spiced
    jam – if you prefer it hotter,
    simply add more chillies.

(V)

Put the chillies/chiles, garlic and ginger in a food processor and blitz until finely chopped.

Put the sugars and vinegar in a large saucepan and cook over a low heat until the sugar has dissolved. Add the chilli/chile mixture, peppers and tomatoes and bring to the boil. Turn the heat down to medium and cook for 45 minutes – 1½ hours, until the mixture darkens in colour and reaches a syrupy, glossy consistency with bubbles like lava. The cooking time will depend on the hob/stove and pan that you are using. Stir the mixture regularly, especially towards the end of the cooking time, so that it does not burn. Be careful when you stir the mixture as it will bubble up, so make sure you do not fill the pan too full.

To test if the jam will be thick enough once it's cooled, put some saucers in the fridge to cool. When you think the jam is ready, put a small teaspoon of jam on a cold saucer; leave it for a minute, then dip your finger in it to check the consistency.

To sterilize your jam jars, preheat the oven to 120°C (250°F) Gas ½. Wash the jars thoroughly in hot soapy water then put them on a baking sheet in the oven for about 20 minutes.

When the jam has reached the desired consistency, add some soy sauce and cook for another minute, then remove from the heat. Let the jam sit for 5 minutes. Skim off any scum and then bottle the jam while it is still warm into the warm, sterilized jars leaving a gap at the top of each jar. Seal the jar immediately and store in a cool dry place until ready to eat. If the jar has been properly sterilized, it will keep for 6 months to 1 year.

soups
and salads

Soups and salads are a fantastic way to
showcase fresh vegetables – from light
and refreshing summer dishes to warming
winter comfort food. What better way is
there to enjoy the best seasonal produce
all year round?

roasted tomato and red pepper soup with cheese scones

With its rich colour and depth of flavour, this simple soup is guaranteed to please every time. Served without the scones, this is a vegan recipe.

2 medium red onions, quartered

2 garlic cloves, unpeeled

5 plum tomatoes, halved

4 red bell peppers, halved and deseeded

2 tablespoons olive oil

300 ml/1¼ cups vegetable stock

a pinch of sugar

400-g/14-oz. can chopped tomatoes

salt and freshly ground black pepper

For the cheese scones

250 g/scant 2 cups self-raising/ rising flour, plus extra for dusting

⅓ teaspoon salt

55 g/¼ cup butter

30 g/⅓ cup grated mature/sharp cheddar

1 egg, beaten

130 ml/½ cup semi-skimmed/ 2% milk

1 egg, lightly beaten, to glaze

To serve

1 tablespoon finely chopped fresh basil (optional)

4–6 teaspoons of crème fraîche or sour cream (optional)

a baking sheet, lightly floured

a fluted scone/biscuit cutter

Serves 4–6

(V)

Preheat the oven to 200°C (400°F) Gas 6.

To make the soup, put the onions, garlic, tomatoes and peppers on a greased baking sheet. Sprinkle with the olive oil and salt and pepper and bake for about 30 minutes until the onions and tomatoes are soft and the peppers slightly coloured. Check the garlic after 10–15 minutes and remove from the oven when soft.

Put the peppers in a sealed plastic bag or wrap in clingfilm/plastic wrap and let them cool. Remove the skins from the tomatoes and reserve the flesh in a bowl. Squeeze out the garlic cloves from their skins into the same bowl. Remove any crisp skin from the onions and add the flesh to the garlic and tomatoes.

When the peppers are cool enough to handle, gently remove the skin and put the flesh in the bowl with the other ingredients and add the stock, sugar, canned tomatoes, and salt and pepper to taste. Blend the mixture in a liquidizer/blender until very smooth. Taste and adjust the seasoning if needed.

To make the cheese scones, preheat the oven to 200°C (400°F) Gas 6. Sift the flour and salt together in a mixing bowl. Rub in the butter using a food processor or your finger tips until it resembles breadcrumbs, then stir in the cheese.

Make a well in the middle of the flour mixture. Add the egg and milk and combine well. Form the dough by kneading gently until just brought together and smooth. Roll out onto a lightly floured surface to 2.5 cm/1 inch thick. Stamp out rounds with the cutter, using a downwards motion without twisting. Brush the scones with the egg and dusting with flour. Bake for 15 minutes until well risen and lightly golden.

Ladle the soup into serving bowls and scatter with chopped fresh basil. Swirl a spoonful of sour cream into each bowl, if liked, and serve hot or cold with the cheese scones on the side, if liked.

curried lentil soup with fresh herb purée

The tasty herb purée adds a light, fresh touch to this comforting soup, making it a dish to curl up with all year round.

1 tablespoon vegetable oil
2 shallots, finely chopped
4 garlic cloves, crushed
1 fresh red chilli/chile, finely
    chopped
2 teaspoons turmeric
½ teaspoon garam masala
1 medium sweet potato, chopped
250 g/1⅓ cups dried red split lentils,
    rinsed and drained
500 ml/2 cups vegetable stock
1 tablespoon extra virgin olive oil
salt and freshly ground black pepper
chunks of crusty bread, to serve
    (optional)

For the fresh herb purée
1 tomato
1 garlic clove
2 cm/¾ inch fresh ginger, peeled
1 fresh red chilli/chile
a handful of fresh coriander/cilantro
1 tablespoon vegetable oil

Serves 4–6

To make the soup, heat the vegetable oil in a saucepan set over a low heat and add the shallots. Cover and cook gently for about 5–10 minutes until the shallots have softened but have not taken on any colour. Add the garlic, chilli/chile and spices and cook for 2 minutes. Add the sweet potato and lentils and stir until well incorporated. Pour in enough stock to cover the ingredients. Bring to the boil, then cover and simmer over a low heat for 45–60 minutes, until the lentils and potatoes are very soft.

For a smooth soup, give the mixture a good stir to break down the lentils. Season generously with salt and pepper and stir the extra virgin olive oil through the soup.

To make the herb purée, put all the ingredients in a food processor and blitz until they form a smooth paste. Ladle into serving bowls and swirl a spoonful of herb purée into each bowl. Serve hot with chunks of crusty bread

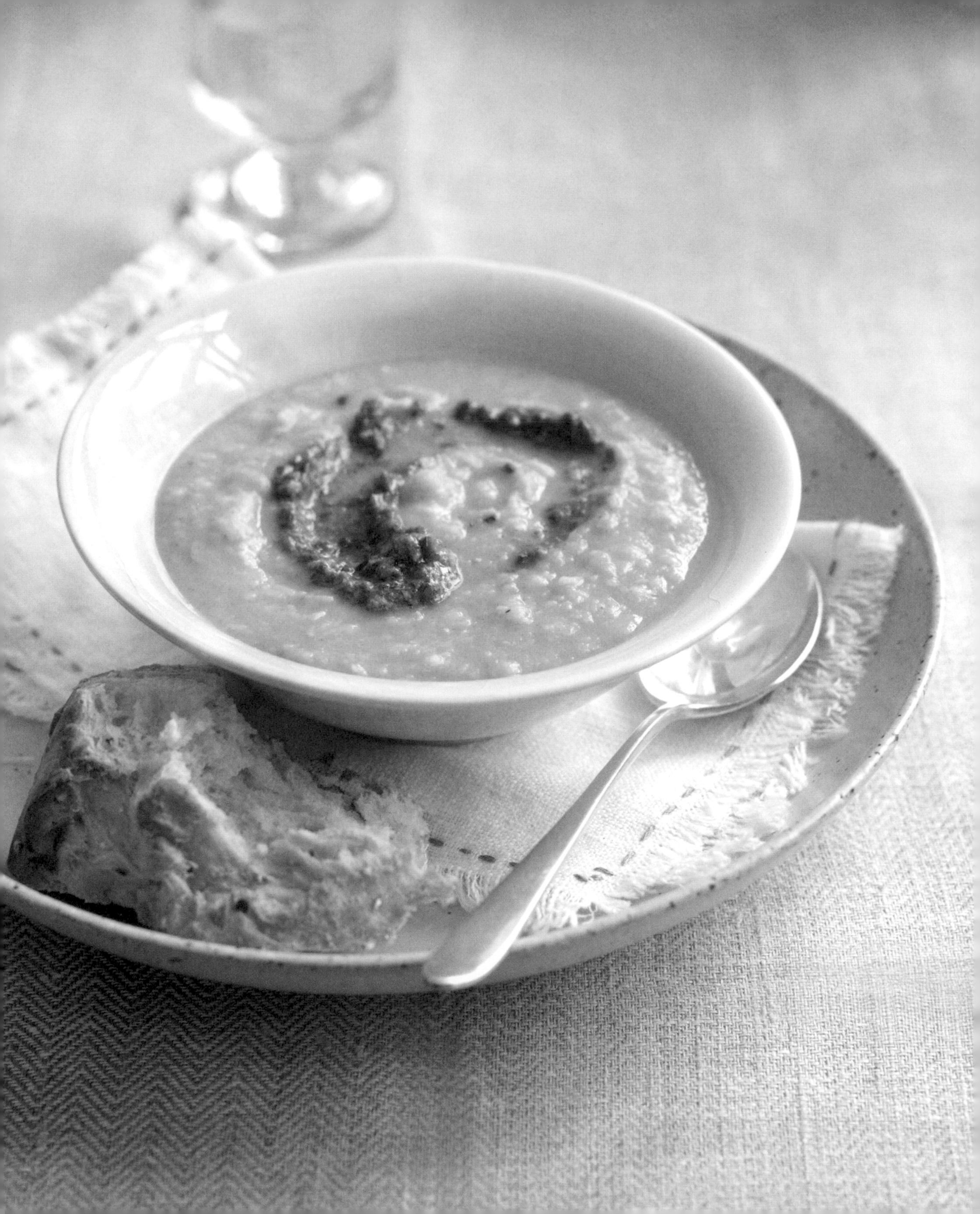

chilled mint and cucumber soup with parmesan crisps

This refreshing, chilled soup is perfect for a warm summer's day. If you are not a fan of chilled soups, we urge you to give this recipe a try and be converted. It is easy to make in advance and will keep for a day in the fridge, ready to serve. The Parmesan crisps add extra texture but are optional.

6 English cucumbers, peeled, cores removed, and flesh chopped into chunks
a small handful of fresh mint, roughly chopped
460 ml/¼ cup crème fraîche or sour cream
freshly grated zest of 1 lemon and freshly squeezed lemon juice, to taste
1½ garlic cloves, crushed
1 teaspoon sugar
salt and freshly ground black pepper

For the Parmesan crisps (optional)
50 g/1¾ oz. Parmesan, finely grated

Serves 4—6

To make the cucumber soup, put the cucumber and mint in a food blender and blitz to a purée. Push the purée through a fine mesh sieve/strainer using the back of a ladle — it will look quite watery.

Put half of the pulp left in the sieve/strainer back into the blender along with the watery mixture. Add the crème fraîche/sour cream, lemon zest, garlic, sugar and salt and pepper, then blitz until combined. Taste the mixture and season with lemon juice, sugar and salt and pepper. This soup needs to be highly seasoned to bring out the delicate flavours.

Preheat oven at 180°C (350°F) Gas 4.

To make the Parmesan crisps, spread thin strips of grated Parmesan on a baking sheet lined with parchment paper. Ensure you leave a good space between each strip as they will spread in the oven.

Bake in the oven for 7 minutes until the Parmesan melts and colours slightly. Remove from the oven and gently remove the crisps from the baking sheet using a palette knife. Put the crisps on a cooling rack until cooled and crisp.

Ladle the soup into serving bowls and put an ice cube in each bowl of soup to keep well chilled. Top with the Parmesan crisps and serve immediately.

roasted vegetable salad with grilled halloumi, rocket and basil oil

A fresh and colourful salad that is quick and easy to prepare — perfect for a mid-week meal. Simply chop your preferred vegetables and roast them in the oven for 40 minutes while you put your feet up at the end of a long day.

3 tablespoons olive oil
2 red onions, peeled and quartered
1 aubergine/eggplant, cut into chunks
1 courgette/zucchini, cut into chunks
1 sweet potato, cut into chunks
1 red bell pepper, sliced into strips
a handful of cherry tomatoes
4 garlic cloves, unpeeled
250 g/9 oz. halloumi, sliced into strips
140 g/5 oz. rocket/arugula (about 2½ cups)
a small handful of toasted pine nuts
salt and freshly ground black pepper

For the basil oil
a small handful of basil leaves
100 ml/⅓ cup olive oil

Serves 4

Preheat the oven to 200°C (400°F) Gas 6.

Put the vegetables in a large roasting pan with the olive oil. Season well with salt and pepper. Roast the vegetables for 40–60 minutes, until they are soft and golden but still holding their shape.

To make the basil oil, bring a small saucepan of water to the boil. Put the basil leaves in the boiling water for just 10 seconds. Remove them and dip in a bowl of cold water to cool. Drain and dry the basil leaves, then put them in a food processor and set the motor running. Drizzle in the olive oil then strain the mixture into a bowl and set aside.

Lightly oil a stovetop griddle/grill pan or frying pan/skillet and set over medium heat. Lay the strips of halloumi in the pan and cook until they turn golden brown, turning half way through cooking.

To assemble the salad, stir the rocket/arugula through the roasted vegetables. Peel the garlic cloves and add to the salad. Spoon the salad onto a serving plate and top with the halloumi. Drizzle with the basil oil and sprinkle over the pine nuts. Serve immediately.

beetroot, quinoa and green bean salad with spicy ginger dressing and shallot crisps

This exotic salad uses quinoa, an excellent, gluten-free alternative to staples such as couscous. Quinoa is a great addition to a vegetarian diet as it is a complete protein source and very rich in fibre. For an extra crunchy texture, sprinkle the salad with shallot crisps — they make a great topping for soups too.

2 raw beetroot/beets, skin on
a large handful of green beans
100 g/1 cup quinoa
250 ml/1 cup vegetable stock
a handful of toasted pistachios
200 g/1½ cups canned chickpeas
2 oranges, peeled and sliced into
    thin rounds

For the shallot crisps
1 shallot, finely sliced
3 tablespoons seasoned
    gram/chickpea flour
vegetable oil for frying

For the spicy ginger dressing
grated zest and freshly squeezed
    juice of ½ an orange
freshly squeezed juice of ½ a lemon
1 garlic clove, crushed
2-cm/¾-inch piece of fresh ginger,
    finely chopped or grated
½–1 fresh red chilli/chile,
    finely diced
a handful of fresh mint, finely
    chopped
salt and freshly ground black pepper

Serves 2–4

Preheat the oven to 200°C (400°F) Gas 6.

Wrap the beetroot/beets in kitchen foil and roast them in the oven for 30 minutes until they have begun to soften. Allow to cool and cut into bite-sized pieces.

Bring a saucepan of water to the boil and cook the green beans for about 4 minutes until they are just cooked but still have a bite to them. Once the beans are cooked, plunge them into a bowl of cold water to stop the cooking process.

Put the quinoa and vegetable stock in a saucepan. Bring to the boil, then simmer for about 15 minutes until the grains are cooked (softened but retaining a bite) and the stock has been absorbed. Remove from the heat, cover the pan and let the quinoa steam for 5 minutes, then fluff up with a fork.

To make the shallot crisps, toss the shallot in the gram/chickpea flour until well covered. Put 1 cm/⅜ inch of oil in a deep pan or wok and set over medium heat. Heat the oil to 180°C/350°F – do not allow the oil to become so hot that it smokes and spits. (If you do not have a thermometer, the oil is at the right temperature when a small piece of bread dropped into it takes 40 seconds to turn golden brown.) Drop the coated shallot slices into the pan and fry for 30 seconds until they are crisp and golden. Drain on paper towels and sprinkle with salt.

To make the dressing, put all of the ingredients in a bowl and whisk until well incorporated. Season with salt and pepper.

To assemble the salad, put all the ingredients into a large bowl. Toss with the dressing, then serve on plates with a sprinkling of shallot crisps.

summer vegetable carpaccio

In this refreshing carpaccio, the nearly transparent slices of vegetable are enhanced with a tangy sour-sweet Asian dressing. You can use any firm vegetable you have in your fridge – the key is to slice them paper-thin so that they can absorb the dressing and tenderize. Using a mandoline-type slicer will ensure neat, thin shaving. It makes a lovely light appetizer or side dish and is just right for summer eating.

5 large radishes
1 large carrot
½ a fennel bulb
1 large courgette/zucchini
½ a red onion

For the Asian dressing
1 garlic clove
2 teaspoons finely chopped ginger
1 tomato, skinned and finely
    chopped
1 tablespoon finely chopped mint
1 tablespoon finely chopped
    coriander/cilantro
grated zest of 1 lime and freshly
    squeezed juice of ½ a lime
3 tablespoons extra virgin olive oil
½ tablespoon rice wine or white
    wine vinegar
½ fresh red chilli/chile
1½ teaspoons granulated sugar
salt and freshly ground black pepper

Serves 4–6

Using a mandoline, vegetable peeler or very sharp knife, carefully slice the radishes, fennel, courgette/zucchini and red onion as finely as possibly. Put the prepared vegetables in a bowl, cover and set aside while you make the Asian dressing.

To make the Asian dressing, simply put all of the ingredients in a small bowl and whisk with a fork until well combined.

To assemble, pour the dressing over the prepared vegetables and toss well to coat evenly. Use salad servers to arrange the salad on serving plates and serve immediately.

winter salad of pearl barley, mushrooms and walnuts

Pearl barley is a great, high-fibre, high-protein alternative to staples such as rice and couscous and has a lovely nutty flavour. A mix of seasonal mushrooms will give this salad a rich, earthy taste while the chilli adds a welcome touch of warming spice on a cold day.

200 g/1 cup pearl barley
400 ml/1¾ cups vegetable stock
a handful of shelled walnut halves
1 tablespoon walnut oil
320 g/about 5 cups sliced mixed
    seasonal mushrooms
2 garlic cloves, crushed
¼ teaspoon dried rosemary
¼ teaspoon dried chilli/hot red
    pepper flakes
a handful of peppery salad leaves
salt and freshly ground black pepper

For the vinaigrette dressing
4 spring onions/scallions,
    finely chopped
2 tablespoons walnut oil
2 teaspoons balsamic vinegar
a squeeze of lemon juice
a handful of fresh flat-leaf parsley,
    finely chopped

Serves 2–4

Put the pearl barley and stock in a saucepan set over medium heat. Bring to the boil and simmer for 20–30 minutes until it is tender but retains its bite.

Meanwhile, toast the walnuts in a dry frying pan/skillet set over a medium heat.

Heat the walnut oil in a separate frying pan/skillet and add the mushrooms and garlic. Fry until golden, then season with salt and pepper. Stir in the rosemary and chilli/hot red pepper flakes. Pour the mixture into a bowl and put the pan back on the stove to make the dressing.

To make the dressing, put the spring onions/scallions, walnut oil, balsamic vinegar and lemon juice in the pan and stir until well combined. Set the pan over low heat and cook until the mixture bubbles. Remove from the heat, season with salt and pepper and stir in the parsley.

To assemble the salad, put the salad leaves in a large bowl with the mushrooms and pearl barley and stir in the dressing. Toss to combine, spoon into serving bowls and serve immediately.

warm curried lentil salad with paneer or tofu and a spiced dressing

This fresh and tasty salad is mildly spiced and perfect with either fried paneer or marinated tofu, for a vegan version. The salad itself keeps well so can be made in advance, allowing the flavours to develop.

400-g/14-oz. can green lentils
2 sticks celery, finely sliced
2 carrots, grated
50 g/heaped ⅓ cup cashews, toasted
½ mango, cut in half and sliced lengthways
finely grated zest of ½ a lime
1 tablespoon vegetable oil
200 g/7 oz. paneer or tofu, sliced
a handful of fresh mint or coriander/cilantro leaves chopped
lime wedges, to serve

For the spiced dressing
4 tablespoons vegetable oil
1 shallot, finely chopped
½ teaspoon mustard seeds
1 teaspoon garam masala
½ teaspoon turmeric
a pinch of dried chilli/hot red pepper flakes
1 garlic clove, crushed
1 teaspoon sugar
1 tablespoon white wine vinegar
50 g/⅓ cup sultanas/golden raisins
½ fresh red chilli/chile, deseeded and finely diced

Serves 2–4

To make the spiced dressing, heat half the oil in a small saucepan. Add the shallot and cook over low heat for 5 minutes, until it starts to soften but still has a slight bite and has not taken on any colour. Add the remaining oil, mustard seeds, garam masala, turmeric, dried chilli/hot red pepper flakes, garlic and sugar, and cook for 2 minutes. Turn off the heat and add the vinegar, sultanas and fresh chilli/chile.

For the salad, put the lentils, celery, carrots, toasted cashews, mango and lime zest in a large bowl. Pour in the warm dressing, reserving about 2 tablespoons to serve, and stir until well combined and coated in the dressing.

To cook the paneer or tofu, heat the oil in a frying pan/skillet and fry the slices until golden on both sides, using tongs to turn half way through cooking.

Brush the paneer or tofu slices with the reserved dressing and serve on top of the salad. Finish the salad with fresh mint or coriander/cilantro, and with lime wedges on the side for squeezing.

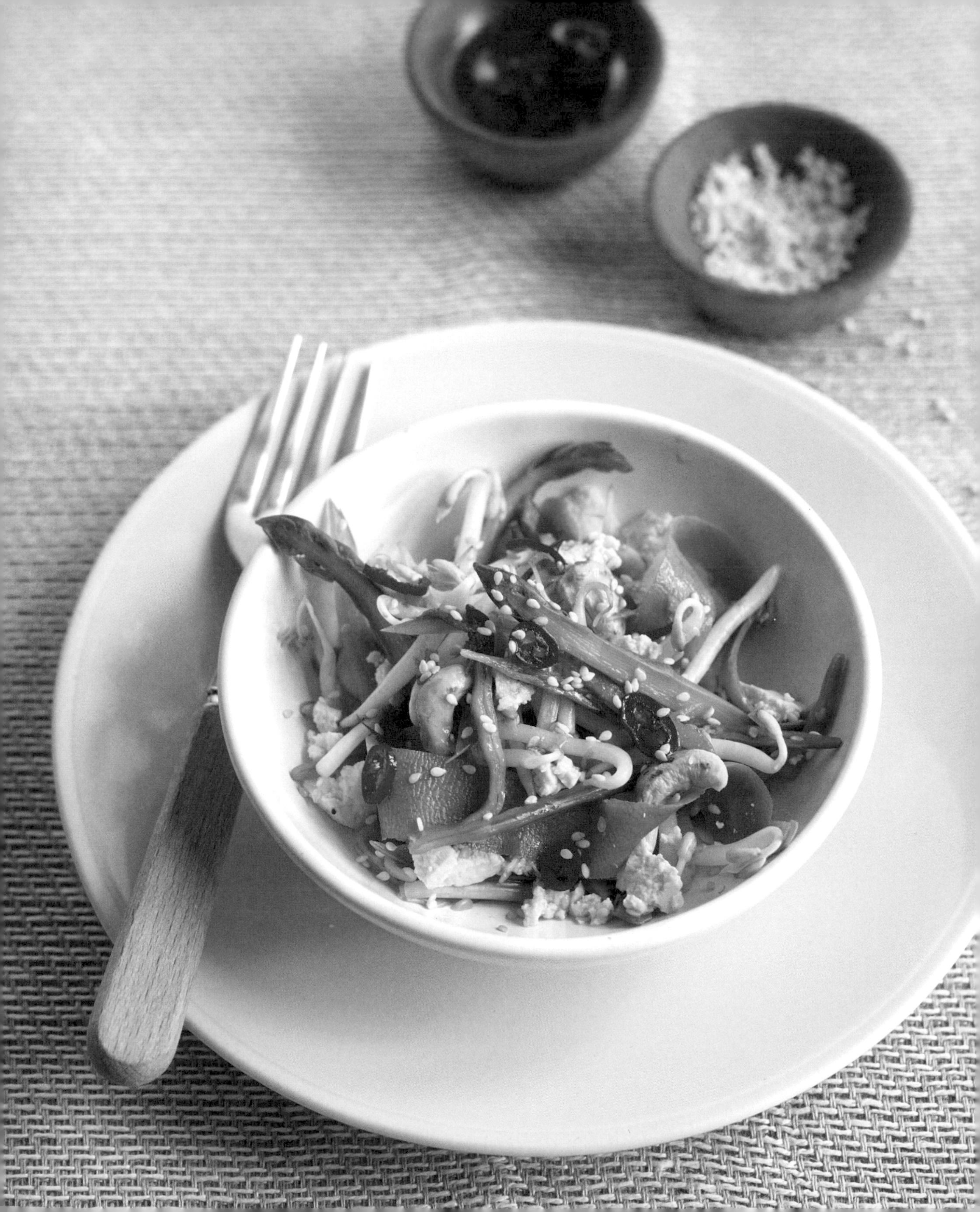

asian-style hot and sour salad with marinated tofu

This crunchy salad is perfect for a light lunch or as a small dish to serve as part of an Asian meal. You can use any fresh vegetables that you have to hand.

100 g/about 1 cup asparagus tips
100 g/about 1 cup mange tout/
  snow peas
50 g/⅓ cup toasted cashews
100 g/2 cup fresh beansprouts
100 g/3½ oz. rice noodles (optional)
1 carrot, sliced into ribbons
1 tablespoon toasted sesame seeds,
  to serve

For the marinated tofu
200 g/7 oz. tofu
2 tablespoons sesame oil
1 tablespoon dark soy sauce
  or tamari
½ fresh red chilli/chile, finely
  chopped
1 teaspoon grated fresh ginger
grated zest and freshly squeezed
  juice of ½ a lime
½ teaspoon sugar

For the dressing
½ teaspoon salt
2 teaspoons sugar
grated zest and freshly squeezed
  juice of 1 lime
1 teaspoon white wine vinegar
½ fresh red chilli/chile

Serves 4

For the marinated tofu, put all of the ingredients except the tofu in a bowl and stir until well combined. Put the tofu in a separate bowl, pour the marinade over it and set aside to marinate for 30 minutes.

Bring a saucepan of water to the boil and cook the asparagus and mange tout/snow peas for 3 minutes, until they soften slightly but still have a crunch to them. Remove them from the boiling water and put them into a bowl of ice-cold water to stop the cooking process. Drain, then slice in half lengthways and put them in a serving bowl. Add the cashews to the serving bowl.

If you are using rice noodles, cook them according to the manufacturer's instructions.

Put all of the dressing ingredients in a bowl and stir until well combined. Place the rest of the salad ingredients in the serving bowl, add the dressing and toss to coat the salad. Crumble the marinated tofu over the salad and finish with a sprinkling of sesame seeds.

italian-style tear and share bread

This soft focaccia-style bread is a great accompaniment to soup or salad. You can add your choice of flavoursome toppings, from simple sea salt flakes and fresh rosemary needles, to cherry tomatoes, red onion and fresh pesto.

450 g/1 lb. white strong/bread flour
(between 3⅓–3½ cups)
2 teaspoons salt
7-g/¼-oz. envelope fast-action
dried yeast
1 teaspoon sugar
3 tablespoons olive oil
250 ml/about 1 cup luke warm water

For the topping
olive oil, for drizzling
several large pinches of sea
salt flakes
100 g/⅔ cup cherry tomatoes
2 tablespoons any pesto of your
choice (page 58), or use ready-
made fresh red or green pesto)
a handful of fresh rosemary needles
1 red onion, thinly sliced

Serves 6

Put the flour and salt in a large bowl and mix together. Stir the dried yeast and sugar through the flour and set aside. Make a well in the centre of the flour and add the olive oil. Then add 185 ml/¾ cup of the water. Quickly stir together to form a soft dough. If the dough seems dry, add the remaining water.

Tip the dough onto a lightly floured surface and knead for about 10 minutes until the dough becomes smooth and elastic. To test if the dough is well kneaded, pick up the dough and fold it back on itself to make a ball. Push the flat of your finger tip into the dough. If the indent springs back, the dough has been sufficiently kneaded and is ready rise.

Put the dough back in the bowl and cover with oiled clingfilm/plastic wrap. Leave it to rise in a warm place for about 45 minutes until doubled in size. To test whether the dough has risen, make another indent in the dough. If the indent remains and the dough does not spring back, it is ready.

Knock back/punch down your dough by kneading for 1–2 minutes. Sprinkle some flour on a baking sheet and stretch out your dough into a large rectangle, about 2 cm/¾ inch thick. Cover with oiled clingfilm/plastic wrap and set aside to prove/rise for about 30–40 minutes. When the dough is ready, it will have doubled in size and, if you make an indent, it will spring back half way.

Preheat the oven to 200°C (400°F) Gas 6.

Use a finger to dimple the top of the dough all over — press your finger into the dough to make regular indents until the whole loaf is a mass of dimples, then sprinkle the bread with olive oil and salt flakes. Add the cherry tomatoes, pesto and rosemary. Bake in the top of the oven for 25–30 minutes in total, sliding it out of the oven after 10 minutes just to quickly add the onion. It should be fairly well risen and golden brown and feel quite light when you pick it up, and have a hollow sound to it when you tap the bottom.

simple soda bread

Soda bread is quick and simple to make and a welcome treat, served as an accompaniment to homemade soup. It can be ready in as little as 30 minutes and makes your kitchen smell wonderful, which is a bonus!

175g/1⅓ cups plain/all-purpose white flour
175g/1⅓ cup wholemeal/ wholewheat flour
1 teaspoon salt
1 teaspoon bicarbonate of soda/baking soda
50 g/½ cup porridge/rolled oats
50 g/3½ tablespoons butter
285 ml/1¼ cups buttermilk
a handful of mixed seeds and flour, for topping

Makes 6–8 servings

Preheat the oven to 200°C (400°F) Gas 6.

Sift the flours into a bowl and add the salt, bicarbonate of soda/baking soda and oats. Stir the dry ingredients until they are well combined.

Melt the butter and add it to the buttermilk. Make a well in the centre of the dry ingredients. Pour in the buttermilk and stir the mixture well until all of the dry ingredients are fully incorporated.

Knead the dough with your hands for 1–2 minutes and then use your hands to form it into a round on a baking sheet. Cut a deep cross in the top, then sprinkle the top with some mixed seeds and flour.

Bake in the top of the oven for 20–25 minutes until the loaf is well risen and golden and sounds hollow when tapped on the bottom.

main dishes

Here you'll find delicious no-fuss recipes for
midweek meals and indulgent ideas for the
weekend, when you have more time to spend
in the kitchen. Choose from hearty one-pot
dishes or lighter options for warmer days.

winter vegetable stew with herbed dumplings

This stew is packed with root vegetables making it both hearty and healthy. The recipe is very versatile so use whatever vegetables you have to hand. The vegetables below are perfect for a cold winter's day but in summer, you could replace these with fresh broad/fava beans, peas and asparagus.

2 tablespoons olive oil
25 g/2 tablespoons butter
3 shallots, quartered
2 white potatoes, cut into chunks
1 parsnip, cut into chunks
250 g/9 oz. baby chantenay carrots, left whole
250 g/4 cups button mushrooms
1 leek, sliced into rings
2 garlic cloves, crushed
4 sprigs fresh thyme
1 teaspoon Dijon mustard
2 tablespoons plain/all-purpose flour
1 tablespoon balsamic vinegar
240 ml/1 cup white wine
1 x 400-g/14-oz. can butter beans
250 g/9 oz. fresh raw beetroot/beets, peeled and cut into chunks
300 ml/1¼ cups vegetable stock
salt and freshly ground black pepper

For the herbed dumplings
250 g (2 cups minus 1½ tablespoons) plain/all-purpose flour
2 teaspoons baking powder
125 g (1 stick plus 1 tablespoon) salted butter, chilled
a handful of fresh herbs
pinch of mustard powder (optional)
salt and freshly ground black pepper

Serves 4

Preheat the oven to 180°C (350°F) Gas 4.

Put the oil and butter in a flameproof casserole dish set over a medium heat. Add the shallots and cook for 2 minutes. Add the potatoes, parsnip, carrots, mushrooms and leek and cook for 5 minutes over a medium-high heat, stirring occasionally, until the vegetables start to turn golden. Turn the heat down slightly and add the garlic and thyme. Season generously with salt and pepper, then stir in the mustard. Add the flour and stir until the vegetables are well coated and the flour has disappeared. Add the vinegar and wine and cook for 2 minutes. Add the butter beans and beetroot/beets, stir gently, then add the vegetable stock.

Bring the mixture to the boil and boil for 2 minutes. Then cover the pot with a lid and transfer to the oven. Bake for 40–50 minutes. If the casserole is too liquid at the end of cooking, put it back on the stove and bring it to the boil to reduce the liquid slightly.

Meanwhile, prepare the dumplings. Sift the flour and baking powder into a bowl.

Chop the cold butter into small pieces, then rub it into the flour as if you were making pastry dough. When the mixture looks like breadcrumbs and there are no lumps of butter, stir in the chopped herbs, mustard powder, if using, and season with salt and pepper Add a couple of tablespoons of water, or enough to bring the mixture together to form a stiff dough.

Divide the dough into walnut-sized balls. Cover with clingfilm/plastic wrap and chill in the refrigerator until the stew is cooked. When the stew is ready, put the dumplings on the top of the stew so that they are half submerged. Cover with a lid and return the stew to the oven or put the casserole on the hob/stove over a low-medium heat, and cook for 20 minutes until the dumplings have puffed up and are golden on the top.

carrot and leek tarte tatin

A savoury tarte tatin is a really simple way to make an impressive vegetarian centrepiece, perfect for entertaining. Our favourite recipe uses carrot and leek but would be equally good with sweet roasted tomatoes or shallots.

1 tablespoon olive oil
25 g/2 tablespoons butter
1 tablespoon honey
1 garlic clove, crushed
1-cm/⅜-inch piece of fresh ginger, peeled and finely chopped
1 teaspoon balsamic vinegar
400-g/14-oz. bunch of carrots (about 12 small), scrubbed and left whole
1 leek, cut lengthways into strips
2 tablespoon white wine
375 g/13 oz. ready-rolled puff pastry dough, defrosted if frozen
salt and freshly ground black pepper

For the balsamic reduction
150 ml/⅔ cup balsamic vinegar
50g/¼ cup dark brown sugar
1 tablespoon honey

Serves 4

Preheat the oven to 200°C (400°F) Gas 6.

Put the oil and butter in a large frying pan/skillet with an ovenproof handle and set over medium heat. Add the honey and cook until it bubbles and starts to turn golden brown. Add the garlic, ginger and balsamic vinegar, then lay the carrots in the pan. Roll the carrots around to coat them in the mixture, then top with the leek, using the leek strips to fill in any gaps. Add the white wine, cover with a lid and cook over medium heat for 5 minutes. Uncover and cook for another minute over a high heat until the carrots are golden brown on the underside. Season generously with salt and pepper.

Cut the puff pastry roughly to the size of the pan and place it on top of the carrots and leeks, tucking the edges down the side of the pan. Put the pan in the preheated oven for 20 minutes until the puff pastry is well risen and golden brown.

Meanwhile, prepare the balsamic reduction. Put the balsamic vinegar in a saucepan set over a high heat and boil until it is has reduced by half. Turn down the heat. Add the brown sugar and honey and stir until dissolved. Bring the mixture to a simmer and cook until the mixture is glossy and syrupy.

When the tart is cooked, run a knife around the edge of the pan and turn the tart out, upside-down, onto a warm plate while it is still hot. Drizzle the tart with the balsamic reduction and serve.

vegetable and lentil moussaka

Packed with flavour, this satisfying dish makes a welcome change from lasagne. It can be made ahead of time and is always a crowd pleaser.

2 aubergines/eggplants, sliced lengthways
5 tablespoons olive oil
1 red onion, finely chopped
120 ml/½ cup white wine
1 carrot, finely chopped
1 red bell pepper, finely chopped
½ courgette/zucchini, finely chopped
a handful of dill, finely chopped
1 teaspoon dried oregano
1 teaspoon ground cinnamon
100 g/½ cup red lentils
1 x 400-g/14-oz. can chopped plum tomatoes
600 g/1 lb 5 oz. potatoes, peeled and sliced
400 g/about 2 cups plain yogurt
2 eggs
zest of 1 unwaxed lemon
freshly grated nutmeg
60 g/½ cup crumbled feta cheese
salt and freshly ground black pepper

Serves 4

Preheat the oven to 180°C (350°F) Gas 4.

Sprinkle the aubergine/eggplants with salt and 2 tablespoons olive oil and bake in the preheated oven for 15–20 minutes, until soft and starting to brown.

Meanwhile, put the onion in a large saucepan with 1 tablespoon olive oil and 1 tablespoon water. Cover and cook over low heat for 5–10 minutes until the onion softens without taking on any colour. Take off the lid, add the wine and boil over high heat until the wine has reduced by half. Add the carrot, bell pepper, courgette/zucchini, dill, oregano, and cinnamon and fry until they turn golden brown. Add the lentils and tomatoes, along with 240 ml/1 cup of water and simmer over low heat for 20 minutes. Season with salt and pepper, to taste.

Fry the potatoes in the remaining 2 tablespoons olive oil until they are golden on either side and the potato has started to soften. Remove from the pan and drain on paper towels.

To assemble the moussaka, lay half of the aubergine/eggplant on the bottom of an ovenproof dish, cover with half of the lentil mixture and top with half of the potatoes. Repeat.

To make the topping, whisk the yogurt with the eggs, lemon, nutmeg and half of the feta. Pour on top of the moussaka and sprinkle the top with the remaining crumbled feta. Bake in the oven for 45 minutes until the top is golden brown. Serve hot or at room temperature with a green salad.

beetroot risotto

A risotto is a great staple for everyday eating. This simple recipe is particularly tasty and its incredible colour will always be a conversation point too!

500 g/18 oz. raw beetroot/beets
2 teaspoons butter
2 red onions, finely chopped
2 garlic cloves, crushed
6–8-cm/2½–3-inch piece of fresh
   ginger, peeled and grated
400 g (2 cups) risotto rice
200 ml (¾ cup plus 1 tablespoon)
   white wine
850 ml/3½ cups vegetable stock
zest and freshly squeezed juice of
   1–2 lemons, to taste
50 g/½ cup grated Parmesan
3 sprigs thyme, leaves finely chopped
a handful of flat-leaf parsley, finely
   chopped, plus extra to serve
salt and freshly ground black pepper

Serves 4

Preheat the oven to 200°C (400°F) Gas 6.

Individually wrap the beetroot/beets in kitchen foil and put them on a baking sheet. Bake in the preheated oven for about 40 minutes, or until tender. Set aside until cool enough to handle, then rub off the skin using the foil and cut the beetroot/beets into cubes. Set aside.

Melt the butter in a heavy-based saucepan, add the onions and cook over low heat for about 10 minutes until soft but not coloured. Add 2 tablespoons of water to the pan if the onions are sticking. Stir in the garlic and ginger and cook for 1–2 minutes. Add the rice and cook until it turns opaque. Add the wine and stir until absorbed. Add a quarter of the stock and stir until all the liquid has been absorbed.

Continue to add the stock in stages, stirring constantly until the rice is soft but still has bite. Remove from the heat, then stir in the lemon zest and juice and the Parmesan. Next stir in the beetroot/beet and thyme, and season with salt and pepper. The consistency should be thick and creamy; add additional stock if required.

Spoon into warmed serving bowls and sprinkle with fresh, chopped parsley. Serve immediately.

homemade baked beans

These smoky homemade baked beans are the perfect comfort food to enjoy on a cosy night in. Eat them spooned over buttered toast, with some crusty bread on the side for dunking, or try them with our quick cornbread (page 15).

2 tablespoons olive oil
1 red onion, chopped
2 garlic cloves, crushed
1 tablespoon brown sugar
1 tablespoon black treacle/molasses
1 teaspoon Dijon mustard
½ teaspoon paprika
1 tablespoon balsamic vinegar
½ fresh red chilli/chile, deseeded
   and finely chopped (optional)
1 x 400-g/14-oz. can haricot/navy
   beans
1 x 400-g/14-oz. can chopped
   tomatoes
240 ml/1 cup vegetable stock
salt and freshly ground black pepper
slices of buttered toast, crusty bread
   or Quick Cornbread (see page 15),
   to serve (optional)

Serves 2—4

Preheat the oven to 160°C (325°F) Gas 3.

Put the oil, onion and 2 teaspoons of water in a flameproof casserole dish, cover with a lid. Cook gently over low heat for about 10 minutes, until the onion is soft but has not taken on too much colour.

Add the garlic, brown sugar, treacle, mustard, paprika, vinegar and chilli/chile, if using, and stir until everything is well incorporated. Add the haricot/navy beans, tomatoes and stock. Bring to the boil, cook for 2 minutes then cover with a lid and transfer to the oven. Bake in the middle of the preheated oven for 2 hours. If the consistency is too liquid, put the casserole dish on the stovetop over gentle heat and reduce the liquid to the desired consistency. Season well with salt and pepper. Serve hot with buttered toast or cornbread.

2 tablespoons olive oil

2 red onions, quartered

1 teaspoon each ground turmeric and cinnamon

½ teaspoon paprika

1-cm/¾-inch piece of fresh ginger, peeled and finely chopped

1 red chilli/chile, finely chopped

2 garlic cloves, crushed

grated zest of 1 orange

1 red and 1 yellow bell pepper, roughly chopped

1 sweet potato, cubed

1 aubergine/eggplant, cut into chunks

2 carrots, sliced

50 g/⅓ cup dried apricots, quartered

400-g/14-oz. can chopped tomatoes

1 tablespoon clear honey or maple syrup

400-g/14-oz. can chickpeas, drained

500 ml/2 cups vegetable stock

a large handful of baby spinach

To serve

a handful of chopped coriander/ cilantro stirred into Greek yogurt (optional)

prepared couscous

Serves 4–6

vegetable tagine

Chloe's friend Annabel makes a delicious Moroccan-style stew, which this recipe is based on. It is a very versatile dish so you can use whatever vegetables you have to hand. Serve with plenty of couscous.

Preheat the oven to 180°C (350°F) Gas 4.

Heat the oil in a flameproof casserole dish set over low–medium heat. Add the onion and cook for 5 minutes. Add the turmeric, cinnamon, paprika, ginger, chilli, garlic and orange zest and cook for 1 minute. Then add the peppers, sweet potato, aubergine/ eggplant and carrots. Stir so that they are well covered with the spice mixture and cook for 2 minutes.

Stir in the apricots, tomatoes, honey and chickpeas. Then add the vegetable stock. Bring to the boil and cook on the stovetop for 2 minutes. Cover with a lid and transfer to the preheated oven to bake for 30–40 minutes. When the tagine is cooked, remove from the oven and stir in the spinach.

Spoon the tagine onto serving plates of couscous and top with chopped fresh coriander/cilantro with yogurt, if liked. Serve hot.

roasted aubergine, sweet potato and spinach curry

This simple, light and healthy curry is easy to make and does not require an extensive stock of spices. Serve it with a generous spoonful of plain yogurt, a sprinkling of chopped fresh herbs and some steamed rice.

2 aubergines/eggplants, chopped into bite-size pieces

1 sweet potato, peeled and chopped into bite-size pieces

2 tablespoons olive oil

1 tablespoon ground cinnamon

1 tablespoon vegetable oil

½ teaspoon mustard seeds

1 shallot, chopped

2-cm/¾-inch piece of fresh ginger, peeled and grated

2 cloves garlic, crushed

1 fresh red chilli/chile, finely chopped

2 teaspoons garam masala

2 teaspoons sugar

1 x 400-g/14-oz. can chopped tomatoes

a large handful of fresh spinach, washed and dried

a pinch or 2 of sugar, to taste

a squeeze of fresh lime juice

salt and freshly ground black pepper

a handful of fresh coriander/cilantro leaves, finely chopped

To serve
cooked rice
plain yogurt (optional)

Serves 4—6

Preheat the oven to 180°C (350°F) Gas 4.

Put the aubergine/eggplant and sweet potato on a baking sheet and season with salt and pepper. Drizzle with the olive oil and sprinkle with cinnamon. Roast in the preheated oven for about 40 minutes, until cooked and golden.

Heat the vegetable oil in a large saucepan. When the oil is hot, add the mustard seeds and cover with a lid. Cook for 2 minutes or until they pop. Turn down the heat, uncover, and add the shallot, ginger, garlic, and chilli/chile. Fry for 3 minutes until they start to soften. Add the garam masala and sugar and fry for 5 minutes. Finally, add the tomatoes and simmer for 15 minutes. Stir the roasted vegetables through the sauce and cook over low heat for about 10 minutes, then stir in the spinach until wilted. Taste and adjust the seasoning by adding more sugar, lime or salt and pepper, to taste.

Spoon onto serving plates and serve hot with rice and a spoonful of plain yogurt, if liked.

marinated stuffed mushrooms with creamy white beans

This dish is based on simple, French-style rustic cuisine. Make the mushrooms on their own and serve them as an appetizer or light lunch (perfect for vegans), or add the creamy, mustard beans to make a warming supper dish.

2 garlic cloves, crushed
4 tablespoons/¼ cup olive oil
4 tablespoons/¼ cup white wine
leaves from a sprig of rosemary
4 large portobello mushrooms, peeled, with stalks removed and reserved for the filling
1 tablespoon capers, drained and chopped
a handful of chopped flat-leaf parsley leaves
4 tablespoons/¼ cup breadcrumbs (made from gluten-free bread if preferred)
olive oil, for brushing
salt and freshly ground black pepper

For the creamy white beans
½ white onion, finely chopped
30 g/2 tablespoons butter
1 x 400-g/14-oz. can haricot/navy or butter/lima beans, drained
150 ml/⅔ cup vegetable stock
2 teaspoons Dijon mustard
3 tablespoons single/light cream (optional)
a handful of spinach, finely chopped
salt and freshly ground black pepper

Serves 2–4

Preheat the oven to 180°C (350°F) Gas 4.

To make the mushrooms, combine the garlic, oil, wine and rosemary together in a bowl. Pour this over the mushrooms and leave them to marinate for 30 minutes.

To make the stuffing for the mushrooms, chop the mushroom stalks and combine them with the capers, parsley, breadcrumbs, salt and pepper in a bowl and add 1 tablespoon of the marinade. Spoon the stuffing on top of the mushrooms, gills-side up

Put the mushrooms in an ovenproof dish and bake in the preheated oven for 15 minutes. Slice the baguette and put the slices on a baking sheet, brush them with a little olive oil and bake in the oven 5 minutes before the mushrooms are finished.

To make the beans, put the onion in a saucepan with the butter, cover and cook over low heat for 5–10 minutes until softened but not coloured. Remove the lid and add the beans and stock. Simmer for 5 minutes. To finish, stir in the mustard, cream and spinach, and season with salt and pepper.

To serve, arrange the mushrooms on a plate and serve with spoonfuls of the creamy beans.

spinach and ricotta stuffed onions

Stuffed onions are much easier to make than you might think and can be prepared ahead of time, so ideal for entertaining. We have filled them with creamy ricotta and spinach, but they could also be filled with a nut-based stuffing. Try serving them with our delicious caponata (page 60) on the side.

8 red or white onions
2 tablespoons olive oil
75g/1½ cups fresh spinach,
   finely chopped
250 g/9 oz. ricotta (1 heaped cup)
grated zest and juice of ½ a lemon
½ teaspoon grated nutmeg
pine nuts and breadcrumbs for
   topping
salt and freshly ground black pepper
Caponata (see page 60), to serve
   (optional)

Serves 4

Preheat the oven to 180°C (350°F) Gas 4.

Cut the root off the onions so that they sit flat. Then cut about 2 cm/¾ inch off the tops and peel off the skins. Hollow out the inside of the onions with a teaspoon, leaving the outer 1 or 2 layers. If there is a hole in the bottom of the onion, use a piece of the onion that has been removed to fill it in.

Put a large sheet of kitchen foil on a baking sheet — enough to wrap the onions, and put the onions on top. Season the onions with salt and pepper, drizzle with olive oil, pour in 2 tablespoons water, then wrap to seal the onions in foil. Bake in the preheated oven for 30 minutes until the onions are soft.

To prepare the filling, wilt the spinach in a saucepan set over low heat. Drain off any excess moisture and let cool. Put the ricotta, spinach, lemon zest and juice, nutmeg and salt and pepper in a bowl and stir until well combined.

Fill the baked onions with the spinach mixture and top with a handful of pine nuts and breadcrumbs to add some crunch to the tops. Put the onions on a baking sheet and return to the oven for 15 minutes or until the tops are golden. Serve immediately with a generous spoonful of Caponata on the side, if liked, and a green salad.

lemon and wild rice stuffed fennel with a fresh tomato sauce

This light and fragrant dish contains fresh herbs, fennel and lemon and is served with a light tomato sauce. It can be made ahead of time, then simply finished in the oven — perfect for dining al fresco in summer.

8 fennel bulbs

1 tablespoon olive oil, plus extra
    for drizzling

4 tablespoons white wine

100 g/⅔ cup wild rice

400 ml/¾ cup vegetable stock

3 shallots, chopped

2 garlic cloves, crushed

grated zest and freshly squeezed
    juice of ½ a lemon

60 g/scant cup grated Parmesan

a handful chopped fresh flat-leaf
    parsley, mint or chives

60 g/1 cup soft breadcrumbs
    (or ½–¾ cup dried)

salt and freshly ground black pepper

For the fresh tomato sauce

4 vine tomatoes

1 garlic clove, crushed

2 tablespoons olive oil

1 tablespoon white wine

1 teaspoon sugar

1 teaspoon tomato purée/paste

a squeeze of fresh lemon juice

1 teaspoon balsamic or white
    wine vinegar

a handful of chopped fresh parsley,
    mint or chives

Serves 4

Preheat the oven to 180°C (350°F) Gas 4.

To prepare the fennel, cut a thin slice off the bottom of the fennel bulb so that it sits flat. Cut about 2 cm/¾ inch off the top of the fennel bulb, so that you can get to the centre of the bulb. Hollow the flesh out of the bulb's centre and finely chop the flesh. Set aside. Put a large sheet of kitchen foil on a baking sheet — enough to wrap the fennel, and put the fennel bulbs on top. Season with salt and pepper, drizzle with olive oil, pour in half the wine, then seal. Bake in the preheated oven for about 40 minutes, until the fennel is soft.

Put the wild rice in a saucepan with the vegetable stock and cook according to the package instructions. Meanwhile, heat 1 tablespoon of the olive oil in a frying pan/skillet. Add the shallots and cook over low heat for 5–10 minutes until softened but not coloured. When cooked, remove half the shallots and set aside. Add the reserved fennel, garlic, lemon zest and juice, the remaining wine and season with salt and pepper. Cover and simmer over low heat until the fennel is soft, then turn up the heat until all the liquid has evaporated and the vegetables turn golden.

Add the cooked rice and half the Parmesan and season with salt and pepper. Finish with chopped fresh herbs. Fill the fennel bulbs with the rice mixture and top with the breadcrumbs, some chopped fresh herbs and remaining Parmesan.

To make the tomato sauce, blanch the tomatoes in boiling water for 10 seconds to remove the skins. Deseed, then finely chop the flesh and set aside. Put the garlic in a saucepan, add the reserved shallots and cook over low heat for 2 minutes. Add the olive oil and the wine. Add the tomato flesh and simmer for 5 minutes. Add the sugar, tomato purée/paste and lemon juice. Stir in the vinegar and herbs. Add a litte water to the sauce to thin, if needed. Serve the fennel warm with a spoonful of tomato sauce on the side.

individual baked cheesecakes with salted honey walnuts

This twist on a classic baked cheesecake is ideal to serve on a special occasion. Use your preferred strong-flavoured cheese and seasonal herbs and serve with a crisp green salad and our Apple, Celery and Mint Salsa (page 62).

For the crust
200 g/7 oz. oatcakes
50 g/3½ tablespoons butter
3 tablespoons honey
salt and freshly ground black pepper

For the filling
150 g/⅔ cup cream cheese
150 g/⅔ cup vegetarian ricotta cheese
75 ml/⅓ cup sour cream
1 teaspoon Dijon mustard
3 egg yolks
100 g/3½ oz. Wensleydale, feta or any blue cheese
a handful of chives, finely chopped
3 egg whites
50g/¾ cup finely grated Parmesan
salt and ground white pepper

For the salted honey walnuts
2 tablespoons honey
2 teaspoons brown sugar
2 teaspoons Maldon sea salt, plus extra for sprinkling
100 g/¾ cup walnut pieces

4 chef's rings, greased

Serves 4

Preheat the oven to 150ºC (300ºF) Gas 2.

To make the crust, put the oatcakes in a plastic bag and crush them with a rolling pin, or whizz to crumbs in a food processor. Tip the crumbs into a large bowl and season with salt and pepper. Melt the butter over gentle heat in a saucepan until the butter foams and turns golden. Remove from the heat and stir in the honey until dissolved. Combine the butter and honey with the oatcake crumbs. Press the crumbs into the bottom of the chef's rings. Use the base of a glass to press down the mixture. Bake the crust in the preheated oven for 8–10 minutes until golden and firm.

Meanwhile, put the cream cheese, ricotta, sour cream, mustard and egg yolks in a bowl and whisk until light and fluffy. Crumble in the cheese, stir in the chives and season with salt and pepper.

In a separate bowl, and using clean beaters, beat the egg whites to medium peaks. Take a spoonful of the egg white and stir it through the cheese mixture to loosen it. Gently fold in the remaining egg whites with a metal spoon.

Cool the oven to 160°C (325°F) Gas 3. Spoon the mixture into the chef's rings to cover the oatcake crust, and sprinkle with the Parmesan. Bake in the preheated oven for 30–40 minutes, until the cheesecakes are golden on top and set but still have a slight, wobble when you gently shake the pans.

To make the salted honey walnuts, put the honey, sugar and salt in a pan. Dissolve over low heat, stirring, until the sugar is dissolved and the honey has turned liquid. Remove from the heat, add the walnut pieces and stir until well coated. Turn the nuts onto the baking sheet and sprinkle with extra salt. Leave to cool and set.

Use a knife to loosen the edges of the cheesecakes and turn them out. Serve warm or at room temperature, with the salted honey walnuts and Apple, Celery and Mint Salsa, if liked.

butternut squash, feta and sage quiche

A basic quiche recipe is a useful thing to have in your cooking repertoire. There are many combinations of vegetables, cheeses and herbs that work well so this recipe can be adapted to suit your chosen ingredients.

For the tart shell
225 g/1¾ cups plain/all-purpose flour
a pinch of salt
130 g/1 stick plus 1 tablespoon cold butter, diced
1 egg yolk mixed with 2 tablespoons milk

For the basic quiche custard
180 g/a good ¾ cup double/heavy cream, or crème fraîche for a healthier option
3 large eggs
1 teaspoon Dijon mustard
30 g/scant ½ cup grated Parmesan (optional)
salt and freshly ground black pepper

For the filling
1 butternut squash, peeled, deseeded and chopped
2 tablespoons olive oil
1 teaspoon fresh sage leaves, finely chopped
80 g/⅔ cup crumbled feta

a 23-cm/9-inch round tart pan

Serves 4–6

Preheat the oven to 190°C (375°F) Gas 5.

Rub the butter into the flour using your fingertips until the mixture looks like breadcrumbs. Sprinkle the pastry with 1½ tablespoons of the egg and milk mixture, stirring it through with a knife. Use your hands to bring the dough together in the bowl but do not knead the dough. If the dough still feels dry, add another ½ tablespoon of the egg and milk mixture. Continue until you can bring the dough together into a smooth, firm dough.

Roll out on a lightly floured work surface, or between 2 sheets of baking parchment, until it is about 3 mm/⅛ inch thick. Use your rolling pin to pick up the dough and lay it over the tart pan. Gently push the dough down into the pan, making sure that the base and edges are well lined. Roll a rolling pin over the top of the tart pan to remove any excess dough and tidy the edges with your fingertips. Chill the tart shell in the fridge for 30 minutes until firm.

Lay a round of baking parchment slightly bigger than the tart pan over the tart shell, pushing the paper down onto the base. Fill with baking beans and bake in the top of the preheated oven for 15 minutes. After 15 minutes, remove the parchment and baking beans and put the tart shell back in the preheated oven for a further 5 minutes, until there are no grey patches and the surface of the pastry has a sandy feel.

To make the custard, put all the ingredients in a bowl and beat together until well mixed. Strain the mixture for a smooth custard.

To make the filling, preheat the oven to 200°C (400°F) Gas 6. Lay the squash in a roasting pan and drizzle with olive oil, and add salt and pepper, to taste. Roast the squash for 30 minutes, until it turns soft and starts to brown. Allow to cool, then stir it through the custard mixture, along with the feta and sage. Spoon the filling into the tart shell. Bake in the middle of the oven for around 20 minutes, until the custard is just set but has a slight, even wobble towards the centre if you gently shake the pan. Serve at room temperature with a green salad.

sweet treats

There is nothing quite like a sweet treat to put a smile on your face and although not strictly necessary for your daily dietary needs, they feed the soul which is just as important! From light fruit desserts and sorbets to baked tarts and cakes, it's time for a little indulgence.

rhubarb, orange and vanilla fool with shortbread cookies

A fool is a traditional English dessert made of puréed fruit and whipped cream. It is very versatile and can be made with any fruit compote. Here, we have replaced the cream with yogurt, which is healthier but just as delicious.

250 g/9 oz. rhubarb, washed and cut into pieces

2 tablespoons caster/superfine sugar

finely grated zest and freshly squeezed juice of 1 orange

2 tablespoons granulated sugar

500 g/2 heaped cups plain yogurt

1 teaspoon vanilla extract or vanilla paste

1 tablespoon icing/confectioners' sugar, sifted

For the shortbread cookies

110 g/½ cup unsalted butter

55 g/¼ cup plus ½ tablespoon golden (unrefined) caster sugar, plus extra to sprinkle

1 teaspoon vanilla extract

180 g/1⅓ cups plain/all-purpose flour

grated zest of ½ a lemon (optional)

a 6-cm/2½-inch round, fluted biscuit/cookie cutter

Serves 4

To make the shortbread cookies, preheat the oven to 180°C (350°F) Gas 4.

Cream the butter, sugar and vanilla until light and fluffy. Sift in the flour, add the lemon zest, if using, and stir it through until the mixture forms a dough. Turn the dough onto a floured surface and roll out to a ½-cm/¼-inch thickness. Stamp out rounds, using a cookie cutter and put them on a baking sheet. Sprinkle each cookie with a little sugar and chill in the refrigerator for 30 minutes until firm. Bake in the preheated oven for 10–12 minutes, then transfer the individual cookies to a wire rack to cool. Be careful as you transfer the cookies, as they will still be soft but will firm up as they cool.

To make the fool, preheat the oven to 200°C (400°F) Gas 6.

Arrange the rhubarb on a baking sheet and sprinkle with the caster/superfine sugar, orange zest and half the juice. Roast in the preheated oven for 15 minutes until tender, then transfer to a bowl.

Combine the sugar in a saucepan with 4 tablespoons water, and set over low heat until the sugar dissolves. Turn up the heat and boil for 2 minutes to make a syrup. Pour the syrup over the cooked rhubarb, add the remaining orange juice, and set aside to cool.

Put one third of the rhubarb mixture in a food processor and blend to a purée. Set aside.

Beat together the yogurt, vanilla and icing/confectioners' sugar. Add the cooked rhubarb and stir to combine. Put a spoonful of the puréed rhubarb in the bottom of 4 glass serving dishes, then add the yogurt mixture, then swirl some more of the compôte through the yogurt. Top each bowl with a little crumbled shortbread and serve with a shortbread cookie on the side.

plum frangipane tart with ginger cream

A frangipane tart is a really versatile dessert but it works particularly well with apples, plums, cherries or apricots. If you don't have any fruit to hand, simply cover the base/pie shell with a layer of jam and top with almond flakes.

For the tart shell
1 Tart Shell (see page 116) made with 1 teaspoon mixed spice added to the flour before sifting and 2½ tablespoons golden (unrefined) caster sugar stirred into the flour

For the frangipane filling
110 g/½ cup butter
110 g/½ cup plus 1 tablespoon sugar
2 eggs
1 teaspoon vanilla extract
30 g/3⅔ tablespoons plain/ all-purpose flour
110 g/1 heaped cup ground almonds
400 g/14 oz. plums, washed, stoned/pitted and halved

For the ginger cream
150 ml/⅔ cup whipping or double/heavy cream
1 tablespoon icing/confectioners' sugar
2 tablespoons of syrup from a jar of stem/preserved ginger
1 tablespoon finely chopped stem/preserved ginger in syrup (from a jar)

a 23-cm/9-inch tart pan

Serves 6–8

Make the pastry dough and prepare and bake the tart shell following the instructions given on page 116. Simply add the caster sugar to the pastry base and combine well before adding the liquid. Turn the oven down to 180°C (350°F) Gas 4.

To make the frangipane filling, put the butter and sugar in a bowl, and cream together until light and fluffy. Add the eggs, 1 at a time, beating well between each addition and then add the vanilla. In another bowl, stir the flour and ground almonds together, then add them to the butter mixture and stir until they are well incorporated. Pour the frangipane mixture into the tart shell and evenly space the plum halves on top, pushing them down so that the edges are submerged. Bake in the still hot oven for 30–40 minutes or until the frangipane is golden, well risen and firm to the touch. Cool on a wire rack.

For the ginger cream, put the cream, icing/confectioners' sugar and syrup in a bowl and whisk until it forms soft peaks and the mixture holds its shape. Add the chopped stem ginger and stir it through the cream. Serves slices of warm plum frangipane tart with a spoonful of ginger cream on the side.

summer berry sorbet with almond tuilles

This simple sorbet is light and fresh, ideal on a warm day or at the end of a heavy meal. Frozen berries are an easy and economical way to buy fruit all year round. You can replace them with fresh berries when in season.

100 g/½ cup sugar
125 ml/½ cup of water
500 g/1 lb. 2 oz. frozen berries
grated zest and freshly squeezed
    juice of 1 orange
1 teaspoon of vanilla extract or
    vanilla paste
a pinch of salt
1 egg white (optional)

For the almond tuilles
1 egg white
25 g/3 tablespoons plain/
    all-purpose flour
40 g/3 tablespoons sugar
25 g/1¾ tablespoons melted butter
a drop of vanilla extract
a handful of flaked/slivered almonds
an ice cream maker (optional)

Serves 2–4

To make the sorbet/sherbet, put the sugar and water in a saucepan and set over low heat until the sugar dissolves. Turn up the heat and boil for 2 minutes to make a syrup. Put the berries, orange zest, orange juice, vanilla extract and salt in another saucepan. Pour the sugar syrup over the top, then put the pan on the heat and simmer for 10 minutes. Set aside to cool.

When the mixture is cool, blitz it in a food processor until smooth, then strain the mixture to remove the seeds and put it in an ice cream maker, following the manufacturer's instructions. If you do not have an ice cream maker, put the mixture in an airtight container in the freezer until it starts to firm up (3–4 hours). Before the mixture is too firm, remove it from the freezer and blitz it in a food processor to remove any ice crystals. Return the mixture to the container and freezer.

To make the tuilles, preheat the oven to 190°C (375°F) Gas 5.

Put the egg white in a bowl and beat it with a fork until it starts to form bubbles. Sift in the flour and stir in with the sugar until they are fully incorporated, then add the melted butter and vanilla, and stir to combine.

Put a teaspoon of the mixture onto a baking sheet and, using the back of a spoon, spread it out very thinly so that you can almost see through it. Leave at least 2.5 cm/1 inch of space between the tuilles so that they do not spread together. Sprinkle the tuilles with the almonds.

Bake in the preheated oven for around 5 minutes or until they turn golden on the edges (keep an eye on them as they burn easily). Take the baking sheet out of the oven. Leaving the tuilles on the hot sheet so that they do not cool down, carefully pick up each one with a palette knife or spatula and bend it around a rolling pin or handle of a wooden spoon to shape it. If they become too firm to mould, return them to the oven for 30 seconds. For flat tuilles, simply remove them from the baking sheet to cool.

Serve scoops of the sorbet/sherbet with the almond tuilles on the side.

individual hazelnut meringues with cream & raspberries

This dessert was Jane's grandma's go-to dessert recipe. An easy win, it can be whipped up in no time, or can be made ahead.

For the meringues

3 egg whites

225 g/1 cup plus 2 tablespoons caster/superfine sugar

1 teaspoon vanilla extract

100 g/¾ cup hazelnuts (or pecans or walnuts), very finely chopped or blitzed in a food processor

16 Ritz crackers, crushed

½ teaspoon baking powder

For the filling

300 ml/1¼ cups whipping cream, well chilled

4 tablespoons/¼ cup icing/ confectioners' sugar

50 g/about 2 oz. fresh raspberries, (mango and strawberries also work well)

2 baking sheets lined with parchment paper OR
2 x 15-cm/6-inch cake pans, lined
a piping/pastry bag fitted with a large nozzle (optional)

Serves 6—8

If using baking sheets lined with parchment paper, use a pencil to draw an even number of 6-cm/2½-inch-diameter circles to show where the meringues will go (you will pipe or spoon the meringue onto these).

Preheat the oven 180°C (350°F) Gas 4.

Place the egg whites in a dry, grease-free bowl and, using an electric whisk/beater, beat the whites to stiff peaks. Gradually add the sugar to the egg whites, a spoonful at a time, bringing the mixture back to stiff peaks between each addition. Stir the vanilla extract through the meringue, then gently fold in the remaining ingredients.

Pipe or spoon individual meringues into the circles drawn on the baking parchment, or else spilt the mixture between the prepared cake pans. Bake on the middle shelf of the preheated oven for 25–30 minutes, until the surface of the meringue is crunchy but the centre remains soft and chewy. Transfer to a wire rack to cool completely before filling.

When ready to serve, make the filling. Whip the chilled cream and icing/confectioners' sugar together until just holding shape. Spoon some cream onto half of the meringues, add some raspberries and top with another meringue. Refrigerate until ready to serve.

apple, blackberry and almond crumble

This classic combination of flavours is always a hit. The crumble topping is best cooked separately, so that it is satisfyingly crunchy all the way through.

850 g/1 lb. 14 oz. cooking apples, eating apples or a combination of the two, peeled and cubed
60 g/⅓ cup Demerara (raw) sugar
grated zest from 2 lemons
½ teaspoon ground cinnamon
1 cinnamon stick
½ teaspoon vanilla extract or 1 vanilla bean
freshly grated nutmeg, to taste
360 g/13 oz. blackberries, fresh or frozen (about 2½–3 cups)
freshly squeezed lemon juice, to taste
50 g/heaped ⅓ cup blanched almonds (optional)
plain yogurt or vanilla ice cream, to serve

For the crumble topping
200 g/1½ cups plain/all-purpose flour (or gluten-free flour such as rice flour)
80 g/heaped ¾ cup ground almonds
1½ teaspoons ground cinnamon
a pinch of salt
125 g/½ cup plus 1 tablespoon butter, cubed and chilled
150 g/¾ cup Demerara (raw) sugar
30 g/heaped ⅓ cup flaked/slivered almonds (optional)

Serves 4–6

Preheat the oven to 160°C (325°F) Gas 3.

For the crumble topping, put the flour, almonds, cinnamon and salt into a bowl and mix well. Add the butter and gently rub it in with the tips of your fingers until the mixture is the consistency of fine breadcrumbs — the same result can be achieved more quickly using a food processor. (If using a food processor, pulse the mixture until the desired texture is achieved so the mixture is not overworked.) Add the sugar and flaked/slivered almonds, if using, and stir until evenly combined. Pour the topping mixture onto a baking sheet and bake in the preheated oven for 20 minutes, or until lightly golden, checking and lightly tossing the mixture halfway through.

To make the fruit filling, put the apple, sugar, lemon zest, ground cinnamon, cinnamon stick, vanilla, nutmeg and 4 tablespoons/ ¼ cup water in a heavy-based saucepan. Set the pan over medium heat and gently cook the apples until still holding their shape but have softened around the edges, and the sugar has melted. If the moisture evaporates and you feel the apple is catching/sticking, add a little more water. Add the blackberries to the mixture and cook gently until heated through. Remove from the heat, take out the cinnamon stick and vanilla bean, if using, and discard. Add lemon juice to taste, then stir in the whole almonds, if using.

Divide the fruit filling between individual dishes or 1 large serving dish, sprinkle over the cooked crumble topping and serve with a spoonful of plain yogurt or vanilla ice cream.

poached amaretto peaches with amaretti cookie crème fraîche

This elegant dessert takes very little time to prepare, it is fruity and sweet, with the crème fraîche giving a refreshing cut-through to the flavour. You can make the peaches in advance and store in the fridge until the next day.

300 g/1½ cups granulated sugar (or caster/superfine)

100 ml (⅓ cup plus 1 tablespoon) di Saronno (Amaretto) liqueur

grated zest and juice of 1 lemon

1 teaspoon vanilla extract

4 star anise

6 firm peaches, left whole with skins on

50 g/heaped ⅓ cup pistachios, to serve

For the Amaretti crème fraîche

100 g/1 cup Amaretti cookies, crushed

500 ml/heaped 2 cups crème fraîche or sour cream

2 tablespoons reserved peach poaching liquid

Serves 6

To roast the pistachios, preheat the oven to 200°C (400°F) Gas 6. Place the pistachios on a baking sheet and bake in the preheated oven for 5 minutes, until lightly toasted.

Put the sugar and 400 ml/1¾ cups water in a saucepan large enough to hold the peaches (but don't add them yet). Set it over low heat, and gently stir the sugar until it has dissolved, then turn up the heat and boil rapidly for 5 minutes — do not stir the mixture at this stage. Turn down the heat, add the liqueur, lemon zest and juice, vanilla and star anise.

Add the peaches to the pan and cook over medium heat for 15 minutes, then remove from the heat. Remove the peaches from the pan with a slotted spoon and let cool, but reserve the poaching liquid. When the peaches are cool, you can gently remove the skins if you wish.

To make the Amaretti crème fraîche, combine the Amaretti cookies with the crème fraîche and 2 tablespoons of poaching liquid. (If you do this earlier the cookies will go soft).

Serve the peaches warm or at room temperature with a spoonful of Amaretti crème fraîche, a drizzle of the poaching liquid and a sprinkling of roasted pistachios.

pineapple carpaccio

This makes a refreshing change for a light dessert, with subtle chilli and background citrus, it is flavoursome on its own, or you can serve it with yogurt, ice cream or chocolate-based desserts.

100 g/½ cup granulated or
    caster/superfine sugar
100 ml (⅓ cup plus 1 tablespoon)
    maple syrup
a pinch of salt
a pinch of saffron threads
1 cinnamon stick
1 vanilla bean, halved lengthways
2 star anise
2 red fresh chillies/chiles,
    very finely chopped
finely grated zest and freshly
    squeezed juice of 2 limes
a small pinch or 3 twists of cracked
    black pepper
50 ml/3½ tablespoons white rum
    (optional)
1 pineapple, peeled, cored, and cut
    horizontally into very thin slices

Serves 4–6

Place the sugar in a saucepan with 400 ml/1¾ cups water. Set over a low heat, stirring gently to dissolve the sugar. Once the sugar is totally dissolved, bring to the boil without stirring for 5 minutes until reduced slightly. Add the maple syrup, salt, saffron, cinnamon stick, vanilla bean and star anise. Turn off the heat and leave to infuse for at least 1–2 hours. Strain the syrup, reserve the vanilla bean and gently scrape out the seeds with a knife. Add the seeds with the chillies/chiles, lime zest, cracked black pepper and white rum, if using. Add 1 tablespoon of the lime juice, taste the syrup and add more to taste.

Put the pineapple in a bowl, cover with the syrup and leave for a couple of hours or overnight in the fridge. Serve on its own or with vanilla ice cream.

caramel oranges with honey mascarpone and toasted pistachios

This simple dessert is low in fat, inexpensive to make and gives a light finish to a meal. It is especially good served after our Vegetable Tagine (page 104).

150 g/¾ cup granulated sugar
a handful of pistachios
2 sliced oranges, peel reserved and
    sliced into thin strips
freshly squeezed juice of
    ½ an orange

**For the honey mascarpone
    (optional)**
250 g/1 heaped cup mascarpone
1 tablespoon icing/confectioners'
    sugar
1 teaspoon vanilla extract

Serves 4

Toast the pistachios in a dry frying pan/skillet over medium heat then put them in a clean kitchen towel and bash with a rolling pin to break them up.

Arrange the orange slices on a serving dish.

Mix the orange juice with 200 ml/1 scant cup water in a jug/pitcher or measuring cup, and set aside.

Put the granulated sugar in a saucepan with 100 ml/1½ cups water. Set over low heat and cook until the sugar dissolves. Bring the mixture to the boil and cook until the mixture turns a dark terracotta colour. Do not stir the mixture while it is boiling, although you can gently swirl the pan occasionally. Carefully take the pan off the heat and pour in the orange juice mixture, 2 tablespoons of water and strips of orange peel. Be careful as the caramel will hiss. Stir the mixture to remove any lumps, and pour it over the orange slices. Leave it to marinate for an hour or so.

Beat the mascarpone with the icing/confectioners' sugar and vanilla extract in a bowl and serve with the oranges. Sprinkle over the toasted pistachios and serve.

orange, almond and amaretto drizzle cake

A light, moist and tasty cake which is flourless so great for gluten-free eaters. As this is a whisked sponge/beaten-batter cake, the lightness and rise of the cake is dependent on incorporating as much air as possible. Carefully folding in the ingredients is essential so that you do not lose too much air.

200 g/2 cups ground almonds, plus extra to prepare the cake pan
1 x 240-g can apricot halves in fruit juice, drained (about 1 cup), with juice reserved
100 g/½ cup full-fat plain yogurt
6 egg yolks
180 g/1 cup minus 1½ tablespoons golden (unrefined) caster sugar
1 teaspoon gluten-free baking powder
6 egg whites

For the drizzling syrup
reserved juice from the canned apricots (about 4 tablespoons)
1 tablespoon honey or maple syrup
2 tablespoons golden (unrefined) caster sugar
grated zest of 1 orange
2 tablespoons di Saronno (Amaretto) liqueur (optional)

a 23-cm/9-inch springform cake pan, greased and base-lined with parchment paper

Serves 6–8

Preheat the oven to 170°C (340°F) Gas 3–4. Dust the base of the prepared cake pan with ground almonds.

Whizz the apricot halves in a food processor until they form a smooth purée. Add the yogurt and whizz until combined.

Put the egg yolks and sugar in a bowl and whisk/beat the mixture until it turns pale and light and fluffy. Gently fold the apricot mixture into the whisked egg yolks. Combine the ground almonds and baking powder and fold this into the egg yolk mixture. Finally, using clean beaters, whisk/beat the egg whites to stiff peaks and carefully fold these into the batter until they are just incorporated and there are no big lumps of white. Scoop the batter into the pan and bake in the preheated oven for 50 minutes to 1 hour until a skewer inserted in the middle comes out clean. This cake tends to take on quite a lot of colour so you may wish to lay a piece of baking parchment over the top of the cake after 30 minutes if it is starting to brown too much. The cake will sink slightly as it cools.

To make the drizzling syrup, put the fruit juice, honey, sugar and orange zest in a saucepan set over low heat, until the sugar has dissolved. Once the sugar has dissolved, bring to the boil and boil for 2–3 minutes to reduce the mixture until it is light and syrupy. Finally, add the Amaretto, if using, and taste.

Pierce holes all over the top of the cake with a skewer and spoon the warm syrup over the cake so that it is absorbed by the sponge. Serve the cake at room temperature, with an extra spoonful of syrup. This cake is sticky so best eaten with a fork.

chocolate orange brownies

These rich, gluten-free brownies are a fantastic treat for almost any occasion. Enjoy them with a cup of mid-morning coffee, add them to a lunch box or warm them and serve as an indulgent dessert with a scoop of vanilla ice cream.

100 g/½ cup minus 1 tablespoon
 unsalted butter
150 g/5½ oz. dark chocolate
30 g/⅓ cup cocoa powder, sifted
100 g/1 cup ground almonds
1 teaspoon gluten-free baking
 powder
3 eggs
200 g/1 cup dark brown sugar
1 teaspoon vanilla extract
grated zest of 1 orange

*a 20 x 30-cm/8 x 12-inch cake pan,
 base-lined with baking parchment*

Serves 6–8

Preheat the oven to 160°C (325°F) Gas 3.

Pour 3–5 cm/1–2 inches of water into a saucepan (or the bottom of a double boiler), place on the hob/stove and bring it to the boil, then turn the heat down to low. Put the butter and chocolate in a heat-proof bowl (or top of a double boiler), place it over the gently simmering water and allow it to melt; then leave it to cool slightly.

In a separate bowl, combine the almonds, cocoa and baking powder. Set aside. In another bowl, combine the eggs, sugar, vanilla and orange zest. Make a well in the centre of the dry ingredients. Pour in the egg mixture and melted chocolate, and stir from the centre until well combined. Pour into the lined tin/pan.

Bake the brownies in the preheated oven for about 25 minutes until set all over and coming away from the sides of the pan slightly. If you like your brownies very gooey, take them out a couple of minutes early; if you like them firm, give them a couple of extra minutes in the oven. Leave to cool in the pan before turning out onto a wire rack. Peel off the baking parchment, transfer to a flat surface and slice into squares or bars, as desired. Serve warm with ice cream or keep in an airtight container to enjoy throughout the week.

pistachio, white chocolate and cranberry biscotti

Biscotti are served as an after-dinner treat with coffee or a liqueur. They make a lovely edible gift, especially at Christmas time. Use the recipe below as a basic one, substituting any dried fruits, nuts and spices you already have in your store cupboard to create your own flavour combinations.

125 g/1 cup minus 1 tablespoon plain/all-purpose flour, plus extra for dusting
¼ teaspoon baking powder
80 g/⅓ cup plus 1 tablespoon sugar
75 g/½ cup pistachios
50 g/⅓ cup dried cranberries
finely grated zest of 1 lemon
50 g/⅓ cup white chocolate drops
2 tablespoons white or black sesame seeds
a pinch of salt
1 teaspoon vanilla extract
1 teaspoon mixed/apple pie spice
50 g/⅓ cup dried fruit, such as chopped apricots or raisins
grated zest of 1 orange
1½ eggs (about 75 g/2½ oz.), lightly beaten

a baking sheet lined with non-stick baking parchment

Serves 6–8

Preheat the oven to 180°C (350°F) Gas 4.

Sift the flour and baking powder into a large mixing bowl, add the other ingredients apart from the egg and mix well to combine.

Add half the egg to the flour mixture and combine using a spoon, gradually adding a little more egg at a time until you can bring the mixture together as a dough with your hand. The dough should be soft and not too sticky. Divide the dough into 3 balls of equal size, lightly flour the work surface and roll each ball into a sausage about 2.5 cm/1 inch across.

Put the dough sausages on the prepared baking sheet with at least 6 cm/2½ inches between them (they spread considerably) and gently flatten the top with your fingers or the back of a fork. Bake in the preheated oven for 20–30 minutes until lightly golden brown. Remove from the baking sheet and place on a wire rack to cool for 10–15 minutes, in which time they will firm up.

Reduce the oven temperature to 140°C (280°F) Gas 1.

Once the biscotti have firmed up, cut into diagonal pieces about 2 cm/¾ inches across. Put the biscotti pieces back on the baking sheet and back into the oven. After about 7 minutes, check to see that the biscotti are drying out and, if the centres are golden, turn the pieces over. Return to the oven and check after another 7 minutes. Cool on a wire rack and store in an airtight container until ready to serve. Perfect with an espresso coffee or dunked into an Italian Vin Santo dessert wine.

index

authors' acknowledgements

Bringing this book to life has been a fantastic experience and would not have been possible without the talented team behind it. With special thanks to:

The team at Ryland Peters & Small: to Cindy Richards and Julia Charles for the opportunity and advice, and to Leslie Harrington, Sonya Nathoo, Ellen Parnavelas, and Megan Smith for your hard work in bringing the recipes to life on the page.

To William Reavell for your wonderful photographs, to Rosie Reynolds for your beautiful food styling and to Jo Harris for gorgeous props and creating the perfect pantry.

And finally, to our families and ever-willing team of tasters. In particular, to Rob and Rachel and to Jon, for your encouragement, advice and support always.